SHIV K. KUMAR
AS A POST-COLONIAL POET

SHIV K. KUMAR
AS A POST-COLONIAL POET

BIJAY KUMAR DAS

ATLANTIC

ATLANTIC PUBLISHERS AND DISTRIBUTORS

Published by
ATLANTIC PUBLISHERS AND DISTRIBUTORS
B-2, Vishal Enclave, Opp. Rajouri Garden, New Delhi-27
Phones : 5413460, 5429987

Sales Office
4215/1, Ansari Road, Darya Ganj, New Delhi-110 002
Phones : 3273880, 3285873, 3280451
Fax : 91-11-3285873
e-mail : info@atlanticbooks.com
web : www.atlanticbooks.com

ISBN 81-269-0047-4

Typeset at
APD Computer Graphics, Delhi

Printed in India at
Mehra Offset Press, Delhi

PREFACE

Shiv K. Kumar is a well-known Post-Colonial Indian English poet. He has published six volumes of poems and the seventh volume, *Thus Spake the Buddha* awaits publication. He has won the coveted Sahitya Akademi Award for his book of verse, *Trapfalls in the Sky* in 1987. Having thoroughly enjoyed his poetry, I would like to share some of my ideas with the readers. This book is designed as a reference book at the Master's and M.Phil. level.

I shall feel rewarded if this book finds favour with the students and researchers of our country.

Last but not the least, I would like to thank Dr. K.R. Gupta, Managing Director and Staff, M/s Atlantic Publishers and Distributors, New Delhi for bringing out the book in record time.

BIJAY KUMAR DAS

CONTENTS

1
Introduction

Shiv K. Kumar (1921-), an academic turned poet has few peers but not many equals among Post-colonial poets in Indian English Literature. A distinguished Professor of English, a critic of eminence, a Bergsonian scholar, Kumar became an all rounder in creative writing — poet, novelist, shortstory writer, playwright and above all, a great translator in the last three decades of the twentieth century — an achievement that has not been surpassed by anyone in our country. Born into an Arora Hindu family near Lahore, Kumar was brought up in an environment of strict discipline of the Arya Samaj under the guidance of his father, who was the Headmaster of a local school, in the sub-urban town near Lahore. Though he 'grew up among books' (besides his father, his grandfather was also a school master), he was emotionally drawn to his mother whose 'vision of life and perceptiveness,' had helped him to understand life better. After getting his M.A. from Forman Christian College, Lahore, he taught English Literature at D.A.V. College, Lahore. In 1947 after partition he migrated to India (*i.e.*, Delhi) and became a lecturer in Hansraj College, Delhi. He went to Cambridge to do research in English and was awarded Doctor of Philosophy (English) for his thesis *Bergson and the Stream of Consciousness Novel* in 1956. On return to India he joined as a Senior Lecturer in English at Government College, Chandigarh and then as a Reader in English at Punjab University, before becoming a Professor of English at Osmania University, Hyderabad in 1959. Later on he held very high academic positions like Professor of English, Head of the Department and Dean of Faculty of

Arts both at the Osmania University and University of Hyderabad, the Acting Vice-Chancellor, University of Hyderabad, Distinguished Visiting Professor of English at the University of Oklahoma, Norman, at the University of Northern Iowa, Cedar Falls, and aboveall, he was elected Fellow of the Royal Society of Literature of the United Kingdom. If this is the graph of his academic life (which is in the ascending order) the graph of his poetic career is no less remarkable for he has already won the Central Sahitya Akademi Award for his book of verse, *Trapfalls in the Sky* in 1987. Kumar began his poetic career as an Imagist poet extending Eliot-Pound tradition to Indian English poetry. For him the image is the idea. His volumes of poems, *Articulate Silences* (1970), *Cobwebs in the Sun* (1974), *Subterfuges* (1976), *Woodpeckers* (1979), *Trapfalls in the Sky* (1986) and *Woolgathering* (1998) firmly establish him as a post-colonial Indian English Poet. Semantically Postcolonialism means something that has a concern only with the national culture after the departure of imperial power. Like colonialism, post-colonialism is a 'state of consciousness', a crucial stage in the continuum of cultural process and selfawareness of the independent nation. It transcends the two types of imperialism — political and cultural that involved colonialism. Thus, language and landscape, self and other, nationalism and transnationalism have become important ingredients of postcolonialism. In this context the theme of landscape and national identity makes a rewarding study in Kumar's Poetry. In him one detects a certainty of touch that seems to reflect a confidence in the direction and purpose of his writing, as well as an integrity of images of India, style and subject matter. Kumar's imaginative world derives its power to involve the reader from its rich mimetic content while its enduring quality comes from the verbal imagery drawn from many sources. Thus, he grapples with ideas and abstractions, images of men and women on several planes the complex of emotions centering round human activities such as love, sex, companionship and problems relating to his own art. The poet's primary commitment is to the image and symbol through which he apprehends reality. Thus, he elaborates how images come to him in a poem called 'Images.'

Images drafted into action
are always dodgers,
snarling restively
like circus lions
When rudely jabbed
showing their dragon teeth,
brandishing their
monstrous paws.
But images that come down
epiphanically are
like hail on a
placid summer afternoon
from cumulonimbus clouds,
carpeting the streets and pavements
with glossy pellets,
like nacres
that may be threaded
into a rosary of
orphic symbols.

Telescoping of images and multiplied association are characteristics of Kumar's poetry.

Kumar right from the beginning of his poetic career is in search of truth that unveils illusion and his poetry seeks to come to terms with reality that transcends appearance. Kumar is essentially a poet of contemporary reality and a seeker of innocence in a world that has been bedevilled with corruption, violence and hypocrisy. The titles of the volumes are very suggestive and indicative of the mood that went into the making of the poems. I concur with Surjit S. Dulai when he makes a pertinent point in the following words :

"Even a casual look at the titles of his books of poetry — *Articulate Silences, Cobwebs in the Sun, Subterfuges, Woodpeckers, Trapfalls in the Sky*, and *Woolgathering* — reveals the subtlety of perception that lies at the heart of his writing.

Here silences say more than speech and the cobwebs — confusions and mysteries of human existence — stand out as sharper glimpses of truth than the bare light of the sun can show. Mind's obliquities are subterfuges to guard a deep perception of truth against its erosion by prosaic directness and oversimplification. No matter how self assured and happily situated one may be on the outside, one can never overcome the gnawing consciousness of the soul's disquietude. In moments of self-scrutiny when our ears are not muffled, we may hear the woodpeckers of our conscience hammering away at our complacencies. Similarly appearances that pass for reality are traps behind which lie profounder truths, calamitous or joyous, revealed only to the poet's eye. Or these truths are themselves traps waiting to fall on the helpless and the unwary, thus signifying the hard lot of human beings. The title of Kumar's forthcoming book of poems, *Woolgathering*, aptly describes the role of the subliminal in the poetic process (JSAL, 1992 : 11).

It is an irony of fate that Kumar began his poetic career with a poem on death titled, "An Encounter with Death," which was occasioned by the death of his mother. His poems revolve around his personal life - in other words, are born out of all experiences in life. Life is presented not as it should have been, but as it is. There is an attempt on Kumar's part to come to terms with life and reality. And hence, pain and suffering become an ingredient of his poetry. His first volume of poems, *Articulate Silences* contains a lot of short lyrics about contemporary reality which depict the 'horror and boredom of life devoid of glory' in the manner of T.S. Eliot and the 'agony abides.' "The Co-ordinates of Pain" gives vent to the agony of the poet as he seeks to escape from it through the medium of poetry. Thus, he writes :

> This saw of pain,
> Piercing through the tendons of my heart,
> must seek its own notation.

Like W.B. Yeats, Kumar excels in short lyrics and again like the former, he too tries to accept life as it comes. Two major themes of his poetry — love and sex (particularly the failure in love and sex) and contemporary reality (*i.e.*, landscape and national identity) are introduced in the very first-volume, *Articulate Silences* successfully. 'Rickshaw-Wallah,' 'Duty Free,' 'Karma,' "Epitaph on an Indian Politician," "Sounds of Hunger" 'I shall not gaze the moon again' are cases in point.

Cobwebs in the Sun reinforces the themes already introduced in *Articulate Silences* and introduces new themes like East-West encounter and cultural interaction and thereby, extends the range of his poetry. Kumar's fondness for imagery and artistic skill give him the necessary impetus to work on these new themes.

Love poems embody specific Indian imagery and thereby, give a kind of authenticity to Kumar as a Post-Colonial Indian English Poet. Behind his love poems like, "Returning Home," "Married Too long," "To A Young Wife," "My Co-respondent," "A Dark Mood," one discerns the ground swell of frustration in love and failed marriage. In "My Co-respondent" the shadow of Robert Lowell looms large. Kumar seems to be concerned with the dissection of the failure of love in marriage. Kumar's poem reminds us of Lowell's "To speak of the war that is in Marriage." Like the husband in Lowell's poem who 'stalls' above his wife, 'like an elephant' gored by the climacteric of his want, the 'Co-sharer' of Kumar's poem 'rose like some Giraffe.' The opening line 'Not my rival but co-sharer' sets the tone of the poem. The protagonist is confident of his power and is not deterred by his rival's advances. He knows that 'often when she made the gesture/you were the prime mover'. Kumar has the Lawrential tendency to relate passion to nature. Therefore, the protagonist in this poem feels assured of the knowledge he has earned and turns to the painful past and explores the nature of the difference between his situation and that of the Co-sharer. Kumar tries to relieve the past through powerfully evoked images as in the following lines :

While you rose like some Giraffe
I slouched over worms
climbing up diamond-knots of wet grass.

Each night I limped into my lone self
Where the dead croaked like frogs.

('My Co-respondent')

The poem is overworked with images. The poet protagonist sacrifices (or is it a retreat?) the woman to the Co-sharer and leaves for 'pastures anew'. Thus, he says :

Now that I give you the rose to keep
let me pass through the turnstile
into the open fields
where riderless horses whinny
under the red moon

The irony in the poem is implicit. The rival in love is termed 'co-sharer' and the tone of the poem is potentially mocking. The competition in love ends with the protogonist deciding to go away into the open fields, leaving the woman to the 'co-sharer.' Kumar adds a new coinage to lovevocabulary by naming the rival in love as 'co-sharer' which undermines the concept of love by turning it to lust. The ground swell of frustration in love forms the bedrock of the poem.

If love and sex become the nerve-centre of Kumar's poetry, landscape and social customs prevalent in the country form the heart of it. Traditional people in India believe in a holy communion with nature and, therefore, they worship the Himalayas and the Ganges. Many of India's religious rites are performed on the banks of her holy rivers after ceremonial bathing. Aldous Huxley wrote a sarcastic essay on Varnasi in which he ridiculed Indians who took a dip in river Ganges. Like Huxley, a rationalist Kumar could not share the blind beliefs of the masses and instead wrote some satirical poems on these rituals. 'Pilgrimage' is one such poem.

The protagonist of the poem, 'Pilgrimage' describes a pilgrimage in which people from different language groups participated. The opening line, "Not all of us spoke the same language" makes it amply clear. The undertone of irony heightens the significance of the poem. The pilgrimage began though we are not told from where and to which place the pilgrims wanted to go. The hardship on the way due to rough weather and scanty supply of food dampened their spirit. The faith of the pilgrims was in question. As the poet puts it :

> The trees on either side
> would have given us a guard of honour
> had our leader not defiled them
> with blasphemies.

The implicit irony reminds us of the loss of faith which characterizes the modern mind. We have been sceptical living in an irreligious milieu. With the lack of faith in God the pilgrimage turned out to be an exercise in futility. Thus, the poet writes :

> We are out to span the sky's amplitude —
> this journey is merely to stimulate the blood.

Then came the denouement in the form of bardic imperative :

> I was the only one to caution
> that the gods had trapped us
> into belief.

Some of his major themes like East-West encounter, assertion of national identity by re-creating indigenous imagery, the subject of growing old and consciousness of losing physical strength and above all, the awareness of death abound in the second collection of his poetry. With the publication of *Cobwebs in the Sun*, Kumar has triumphantly arrived on Indian English poetic scene and looked forward to greater achievement.

Recognition came earlier than expected with the publication of his third book of verse, *Subterfuges* in 1976 by Oxford University Press, Delhi. Kumar is one of the ten Indian English Poets to have been represented in the Oxford anthology of Indian Poets, *i.e., Ten Twentieth Century Indian Poets* chosen and edited by R. Parthasarathy in 1976. *Subterfuges* which contains 26 poems (9 taken from the two earlier books of verse) is Kumar's Magnum opus. It is here he has discovered his voice and 'words obey his call.' With the extension of thematic range, came the technical accomplishment and Kumar became a major voice in post-colonial Indian English Poetry. Like other leading post-colonial Indian English poets such as Nissim Ezekiel, Kamala Das and R. Parthasarathy, Kumar also made an attempt to write a long autobiographical poem in order to a make a fuller expression of the 'self.' In some of the poems in *Subterfuges* such as 'Broken Columns,' 'A Letter from New York' and 'Walking Down the Avenue of the Americas' — Kumar's exploration of self is more direct and deliberate, though the self he studies is not a disembodied self. In each case the historical and cultural context in which the self-discovery takes place is fully and vividly evoked. In fact, Kumar's private and public worlds are not two different worlds. They are distinguishable in terms of perspective and not topography. His poems, therefore, are best approached as those which explore the human condition rather than the isolated individual self. For Kumar it is as necessary to come to terms with the world he lives in as it is to come to terms with himself (1979 : 131), says G.S. Amur and rightly so.

In 'A Letter from New York' Kumar writes about the East-West encounter and brings out the difference in cultural outlook between a native (*i.e.*, an Indian) and a foreign (*i.e.*, an American). Here the poet while searching for an identity mocks at himself which gives an example of ironic humour in his poetry.

> Questions catapult in the air :
> "Are you a Puerto Rican?
> A Jamaican? A Red Indian?
> I look for the feathers on my skull,
> a band around my forehead
> And mumble, 'No, a brown Indian,
> from the land of Gandhi."

I concur with Surjit S. Dulai when he makes a pertinent point on Kumar's autobiographical poems in the following words :

He (Kumar) writes a long poem, "Broken Columns" in seven sections. He will add five more sections to it and include the whole poem again in *Woodpeckers* (1979). It covers Kumar's life from the age of four through the years of growing up, sojourn in England for higher education, an unhappy marriage and divorce. The one thread that runs throughout the poem is the opposition between the urges that drive a person towards a full and free life as a human being and factors, such as conventional morality, established religion, or a bad marriage that conflict with these urges. Essentially this is a conflict between the erotic impulse and civilization. The subterfuges of the title are the devices that society uses to control an individual. The subject in "Broken Columns" and in several other poems in the collection escapes to freedom by countering the conventional restraints of society with his own stratagems, his own subterfuges (1992 : 22).

In "Kali" Kumar uses a profound religious symbol of killing and creating simultaneously. Animal sacrifice is made before gods and goddesses to satisfy the deity can be taken as a form of superstition prevalent in our country. Kumar lashes out such practices in his poem :

> Beyond the priest's monotone
> a lamb bleats for the knife-edge
> A child clinging to famished
> nipples will die anyway,
> but your nectar is the blood
> that jets from fresh arteries.

The tone becomes sarcastic. In the manner of Eliot's observation that "the way up is the way down", Kumar concludes :

> If the way to create
> is the way to kill
> I have hoarded enough blood
> in my throat
> for all the hyenas to suck from.

The attitude is ironic and ambivalent. Kumar has not only dropped hints but 'whispers result,' as well.

In this significant volume of poems *Subterfuges* Kumar has discovered his voice, submerged and controlled, looking before and after. To read his poetry is to watch an actor enacting his tragic play on the stage — it is to see him inside out.

In *Woodpeckers* Kumar has not only depicted life in its numerous aspects but underlined the horror of death. Here, one finds five new sections of *Broken Columns* added to the seven original sections of it published in *Subterfuges*. Again like Emily Dickinson, Kumar is haunted by death consciousness in this volume. Poems like, "At the Ghats of Banaras" and "Crematorium in Adikmet, Hyderabad" are fine poems on death. J. Birje-Patil makes an interesting observation on this subject :

"*Woodpeckers* is a death-hunted volume and yet death is neither celebrated tragically nor is it used as an excuse for philosophizing. There is no orgiastic affair with death, with the poet's self acting as a catalyst. In *Woodpeckers* death is an elderly gentleman, a father, a neighbour, or even the poet's own prematurely aged self that has one day casually ceased to be a part of the living world. The moment of transition from the living to the dead, the moment that writers of tragedy exploit dramatically, is totally ignored. And yet death is a living thing, it has the continuity of the burning ghats whose dead bodies appear with a fatal regularity" (1980 : 241).

In the manner of Louis MacNeice's "Prayer Before Birth," Kumar forewarns an unborn child who is bound to inherit a decadent world in a poem called, "To an Unborn Child."

> I'm sorry you'll inherit
> this subfusc earth.
> We've just moved into this limbo
> Whose walls are papered with unpaid bills.
> And on each day of reckoning
> I play truant while your mother
> feigns hysteria
>
> Come on in —
> We're waiting.

Kumar's fifth book of verse, *Trapfalls in the Sky* which won him the Central Sahitya Akademi Award in 1987 contains three sections : 'On Native Grounds', 'Under Alien Skies' and 'Genesis.' Kumar gives a distinct touch to his Indian sensibilities in these sections. A poem titled, 'An Indian Mother's Advice to her Daughter before Marriage' is a typical example of how Indian mothers tender advice to their daughters to get in on in married life.

> A man's memory is myopic
> like a sparrow's; once filled up
> he hardens into a bedrock.
>
> And often, at night you may find
> yourself alone, pulling feathers
> out of your pillow. But be patient.
> If he's gone out fishing down the dark
> river he'll be back
> for inspite of his appetite, a man
> cannot swallow both ends of the rainbow.

Like Ezekiel, Kumar is against mechanical performance of rituals. He is in favour of the subversion of tradition and rituals and, therefore, irony becomes a favourite mode in his poetry. Instead of river Ganga cleansing us, we need to cleanse it to get rid of water pollution. Thus, he writes :

> It's only when they are carried down the river of time
> that iron sinks into their souls.
> The waters then get sullied by ritual and dogma-
> ashes and bones,
> wilted floral offerings to the dead,
> and the noontime sweat oozing from the saffron-
> striped foreheads of the crocodiles
> whose yawning jaws chant mantras in some obsolete
> tongue.
>
> May be if someone could dismantle all scaffoldings
> along the mother river's waistline
> and ask the dead to seek immersion
> in other confluences,
> the little fish will then bleach these waters
> for the sun's lasers to probe her limpid groin.
>
> ("Cleansing Ganga")

As a post-colonial poet, Kumar makes an attempt to come to terms with contemporary reality. The picture of the capital city of India (*i.e.,* Delhi) is brought alive in a poem called "O Delhi." To read the poem is to know 'the horror and boredom' of life in this city and it is to see it inside out. Kumar recalls his harrowing days when he landed in Delhi as a refugee. In a 'frigid morning,' Kumar landed in Delhi, which received him with open arms.

> ...I felt redeemed
> as you threw open your gates — Kashmir and Ajmeri —
> to welcome indoors a fugitive from another land.
> I savoured your hospitality.

But this Delhi is no more. The poet, who like Adam inherited 'a new garden' asks Delhi : 'what have you done to yourself?' And then makes a prophesy :

> I prophesy that you too will fall
> like Nineveh and Babylon
> and no new Indraprastha will rise
> from your barren ashes.

Kumar's treatment of the theme of love in terms of the elements of Indian landscape has the poetic reconciliation of the spirit and the country. He incorporates the heat and dust, the sun and flood, the crowd, the sense of poverty and deprivation into the texture of his moods. Images of 'India' are handled with a consummate skill and keenness of intellect in Kumar's poetry. Unlike other post-colonial Indian English poets Kumar writes a number of poems on the West and sees it from the Indian view point. His poetry fits into the definition of post-colonial literature which states that the postcolonial writer writes back (the empire writes back). Two sections of *Trapfalls in the Sky* ('Under Alien Skies' and 'Genesis') are about the West. Kumar's poetry exhibits both 'subversion' and 'resistance' — the two important traits of post-colonial literature.

Kumar's sixth book of poems, *Woolgathering* marks the culmination of all his earlier books of verse and is a remarkable achievement. Here, Kumar gives vent to his memory and desire and makes an assertion of 'self' through dream and reality. Life, love, and death-three eternal themes of poetry are worked out artistically in this volume. The poet has come to terms with the mystery of life and declares in "On Listening to Mozart's Requiem" :

> I know when the wind waves its wand,
> it's time to give up.

The world of human beings is contrasted with the world of birds in the manner of Keats', poem "Ode to a Nightingale", in "Talking to a Bird on my Window-sill", to bring home the agony of life. People may change and smile but the agony abides, Kumar seems to say. Thus, he writes :

> You seem to chirp your way through life —
> never a streak of sorrow
> in your beady eyes.
> You don't know the problems I have to face —
> darkness, rain, nightmares —
> or that cyclone, last summer, that uprooted
> a tree in my compound, demolishing
> a nest that had sheltered my vagrant thoughts.

Kumar's poetry being image oriented, it falls into the category of 'Oblique Poetry,' in contrast with 'Direct Poetry' which yields meaning at the surface level. Kumar's poetry makes sense at the deep level, and therefore, irony becomes an important mode in his poetry. For example, an unhappy marriage and divorce are skilfully worked out through subtle imagery and irony in a poem called, "I Say it on Oath, Your Lordship". As Kumar puts it :

> I say it on oath, your Lordship,
> that I'll speak the truth
> and nothing but the truth.
> . . .
> Speaking out one's mind in an open court
> is always an embarrassment

like the wedding-kiss
under the priest's direction.
So may I use my own language, please
which speaks more through vehicle
than tenor?

I was always subjected to the terrors
of her scimitar-tongue, which hurt me
like a surgeon, doing the stitches
without anaesthesia.

. . .

Your Lordship,
how I have withstood these assaults
on my mind's fragile fortress
But now I pray that this siege be lifted...

No more, Your Lordship —
I close my evidence.

Poems on Indian landscape are integrated with the contemporary life in our society as in "Banaras : Winter Morning," "Dawn break over Khasi Hills," "Musings in a Park" and "Moongazing." Kumar is successful in evoking contemporary reality in his poetry. He has an eye for details and nothing untoward escapes his notice — be it the priest who 'chants louder/for a generous tip' as in "Crematorium at Adikmet, Hyderabad" or the darkness which 'has its own norms' as in "Blackout" (like Ezekiel's darkness which has many secrets that light does not know). Apart from the world, death has also attracted the attention of the poet and he wrote some of the poems on this theme in *Woolgathering.* He has written about the elusive nature of writing poetry and the secrets of sorrow in married life in poems like "To a Young Beautiful Woman Aspiring to be a Poet" and "Twenty-fifth Wedding Anniversary" respectively. He says,

In any case, writing a poem is like breaking
a genie into doing a tantric ritual
Even the Sphinx was struck dumb, not knowing
how to solve the riddle

of clipping the wings
of a wanton smile.

(To a Young Beautiful Woman
Aspiring to be a Poet)

There's the first knock at the door —
they have started to pour in,
each wearing his own anniversary on his painted face
poised to wish us many returns of the day —
or the night of eternal discord?

(Twenty-fifth Wedding Anniversary)

But Kumar is not a pessimist poet. He has not abandoned hope. He does not believe that an affair can destroy the virtue of a man. Thus, he questions :

How could virtue be sullied
by a night's brief affair?

(The Ring)

His forthcoming volume (*i.e.*, his seventh book of verse) *Thus Spake the Buddha* contains 41 poems on a wide variety of subjects ranging from personal loss to impersonal and objective observation of contemporary life and situation. The poet has come to terms with his old age and turned philosophical. He has moved from the possessiveness in life to the renunciation of it. He seeks redemption in life and his later poetry is burdened with the consciousness of regaining innocence in life. Two poems, "Lord Krishna to Arjuna," and "Renunciation," stand out in this volume as an epitome of Kumar's spiritual consciousness. Kumar's "Lord Krishna to Arjuna," reminds us of Eliot's "Dry Salvages" (the third poem in *Four Quartets*), and is imbued with wisdom that human beings wish to acquire in life. When Arjun links the thought of the action with the consequence, Lord Krishna dispels his ignorance. Kumar gives a brilliant exposition of this theme in the following lines :

O Lord.
Can an act be divorced from the thought
of recompense?

That's man's ultimate frailty, O Warrior,
to know what lies beyond the horizon,
to know the end even before the beginning,
to know if the seed would sprout
into a leaf, and the leaf into a bud —
if a traveller would reach his destination
before sunset. No, you'd never know
what lies ahead because I hold this card
close to my chest. Or, to put it differently,
it lies in a sealed capsule, under the ocean's
bed, inaccessible to man. Though I know it all,
for I do the choosing — the epicentre
of the next quake, the point of shipwreck
on the ocean's surface, or the arrow that
would transfix the fish's eye in a water bowl.

I choose the sex in the womb,
the hurricane's direction and velocity.
If man were to know his future,
wouldn't he play god?

The fact is that, as Eliot puts it in 'Dry Salvages,' "For us there is only the trying/the rest is not our business." Kumar makes it plain when he says, "Act in the present, banishing all thoughts of the future." Kumar realises the ultimate truth of life by accepting fate that is irrevocable. So he says (Lord Krishna's words to Arjuna),

Then pick up your bow and arrow, O Warrior,
and fight to set the crooked straight.
Your destiny was etched on your palm
at birth. Just as it was preordained
that I accompany you, like the musk
in a deer's navel — a whisper in the air
that leads a lone traveller through a wilderness.
May be I took the human form solely to commune
with you, as we both find ourselves here
between the two forces, good and evil.
A mentor too realizes himself

through his disciple, like the Creator
seeing his image in his creation.

The last poem 'Renunciation' is the logical conclusion of the truth that has been drawn upon the poet in the previous poem. Pain is inseparable from life. Thus, he writes :

Pain, he has now learnt, is born
in the mother's womb, and ends only
when the ashes are silenced
by a sprinkling of milk.
This happened, more than two millennia ago
when sages lived in cages, in harmony
with the wind, rain, thunder —
and the beasts.

With this Kumar has acquired the wisdom of humility and humility is endless.

Kumar's poetry shows a luxuriant growth and sustained development. There are seasonal changes in his poetry but no violent break with the past. The end is predicted from the beginning and in turn marks the culmination of it. The search for innocence, the pangs of life, the failure in love, the betrayal of women, the corruption in public life, the East-West encounter, the hollowness of rituals, the fear of ageing, the pervading presence of death and the predicament of modern man in an irreligious milieu — all attract the attention of Kumar and he takes all these as his themes in his poetry. He portrays life as it is rather than as it should have been. He recreates the characters in their own situation. There is a sense of immediacy in his poetry, which gives the 'feel' of originality to the readers. It evokes a sense of empathy between the poet and the readers. In sum, I should say that the authenticity in Kumar's poetry endears it to the readers both at home and abroad.

WORKS CITED

Ashcroft Bill, Gareth Griffiths and Helen Tiffin. *The Empire Writes Back.* London : Methuen, 1987.

Das, Bijay Kumar. *Critical Essays on Post-colonial Literature*. New Delhi : Atlantic Publishers, 1999.

Griffiths, Gareth. "Representation and Production : Issues of Control in Post-colonial Culture." *Interrogating Post-colonialism: Theory, Text and Context*, 1996.

Mukherjee, Meenakshi. Quoted "Interrogating Postcolonialism." *Interrogating Post-colonialism : Theory, Text and Context*. Ed. Harish Trivedi and Meenakshi Mukherjee. Shimla : Indian Institute of Advanced Study, 1996.

Naik, M.K. "Echo and Voice in Indian Poetry in English." *Contemporary Indian English Verse : An Evaluation*. Ed. Chirantan Kulshrestha. New Delhi; Arnold Heinemann, 1980.

2

The Making of the Poet

Shiv K. Kumar was at the peak of his academic life as a Professor and critic when he published his first book of verse *Articulate Silences* under Writers' Workshop imprint in 1970. Readers feared the worst imagining his poetry to be academic verse full of allusions and cliches. They turned to his poetry with preconceived notions and even reservations. But as one goes through the pages of his very first book of verse, one immediately realises that the fear is unfounded. Kumar's poetry begins with the experiences of life felt in the blood and felt along the heart. It tells us of the sufferings, pain and agony of human beings in our society, that is bedevilled with poverty and corruption. There is no point in romanticizing life in the midst of harsh reality that compels us 'to contemplate the pool of blood.' Unlike the colonial Indian English Poets, Kumar begins his poetic career with a determination to come face to face with reality and sing not the glory of the past but the agony of the present even if it means the unburdening of something related to his personal life. Hence, his early poetry has a ring of autobiograpical element in it.

Kumar's early poetry could be divided into two groups : amatory and autobiographical leaving aside a few poems on contemporary situation and death. Love or rather the failure in love is a major theme in Kumar's poetry. There is many a Freudian slip in Shiv K. Kumar's poetry. The ground swell of frustration in love and married life (*i.e.*, his first marriage) forms the bed rock of his first three volumes of poetry. Metaphorically speaking 'sex breaks into his vision.' In 'Karma,' the betrayal in love causes frustration and anguish in the heart of both the spouses. As Kumar puts it :

...a tear-smudged face,
peering vacantly at the mad woman
on the pavement below,
arguing vehemently with a lamp-post,
while scraps of scandal,
blown lightly from the litter-box
round the street corner,
flap mockingly against the window-panes :
'He fell for that other woman's
brunette hair, the exuberance
of her blue-veined breasts,'
It's that other man now,
dulled by the incessant patter of winter rain,
watching on his window-pane a lustier
drop chase a mere driblet away.
Who's now computing the veins
on those breasts?

Betrayal in love by the woman is brought out in a subtleway in "Parting." Kumar writes :

Now that it's time for parting.
I shall go and dig up the mandrakes,
tear up the ovate purple leaves,
pull out the forked roots,
grind their human carcases into
a potion to benumb my soul in agony.
As your footfalls fade away
down the stairs of uncertain future,
I'm afraid the invidious smog
may cripple my inchoate buds
not yet ripe to withstand the
onslught of the elements.

The echo of John Donne is unmistakable. In 'Song' (a negative poem of Donne) Donne speaks of 'mandrake roots' to show

how impossible it is to get a child with it, so it is to expect of a woman to be constant in love. While love fades away, the agony abides, Kumar seems to say. 'Waiting' is a step ahead of 'Parting' in which the running away of the woman with a stranger is depicted with a heavy heart. The protagonist imagines his 'woman' to be in love with 'a stranger in town,' and therefore, regrets it.

> All night long I have waited for the door-bell
> to ring...
> And that, I know, will not be
> tonight, for she's surely with
> that LSD's dreamy eyed,
> goat-beared, supple-handed
> stranger in town, who'll touch
> her into the fifth dimension
> that I can only dimly conceptualize.
>
> (Waiting)

Frustration in love due to the frivolous nature of the woman and possessiveness of the man is depicted in the poem, "Before the Beginning" through indigenous evocative images of a picnic scene. This is how the poem is composed.

> Twice the thorny bushes
> leaped forward to bait her sari
> as we rambled around
> on the sandy river-bed,
> and each time, I leaned over her
> slouched body to release the hem
> the deep pools of her eyes held me,
> till something flickered to pother those depths again.
> I arrowed a sprig into the placid
> surface of the river to let it float
> down to eternity.
> but before it could set out,
> a dogged whirlpool swallowed
> it under the jungle of weeds.

It's now time to roll up the picnic basket,
put away the crumbs of bread,
for she is already eye-catching a stranger
on the other side of the beach.

Reciprocated love is peace and happiness, and un-requited love is torment of the flesh as well as the spirit. The reason of love is mysterious. One does not work out love as one does a sum in Algebra, it happens. Kumar seems to hold such an opinion when he says :

I can't tell you why I love you —
I don' t know.
Does the protoplasm choose which
tissues to burst into first?
Does the eagle precogitate its
flight through the darkening clouds?
And where do the frogs go
when the puddles dry up?

('Always A Question')

Evanescent love is the cause of anguish felt by the protagonist when he realises that it is difficult for him to salvage the oscillating beloved. Kumar writes in "Before the End" about such a situation with authenticity that immediately evokes a kind of empathy between the protagonist and the reader :

Before she slithers into
abstraction, down the
slopes of time,
hounded by oscillation
I may yet salvage her
Wanton eyelashes' imprint
upon my cheeks and a
certain manner of
sealing our cerebral wrangles
with an impetuous osculation.

('Before the End')

A negative poem "Walking on Ice" likens the 'oscillation' of the beloved to treacherous ice so that the lover would not be able to secure his foothold on her. Thus asks the anguished lover :

> Won't you relent a little
> so that I could plant my heels
> into the cracked crust of
> partially thawed ice?
> Even slush is safer to wade through.

Faithless love is as slippery as walking on ice and therefore, ephemeral in character and evanescent in nature, Kumar seems to say. The observation is based on reality encountered in life and hence, authentic.

A number of poems in Kumar's second book of verse, Cobwebs in the Sun reinfornce the same theme of love already introduced in *Articulate Silences*. Failure in love takes a new dimension when the protagonist apprehends sexual failure in terms of his incapacity to consummate love. Here, the woman is not to blame for there is no betrayal on her part and on the other hand, the protagonist is getting paranoid about his virility and visualising defeat and failure in conjugal life. Poems like 'Aftermath,' 'To A Young Wife,' 'Cerebral Love' give vent to the protagonist's fear of sexual failure. Kumar successfully executes this theme through powerful evocative images in the following lines :

> After a pneumatic bout of love
> lashing our diabetic bodies
> into a semblance of orgasm
> . . .
> She stirs again
> but I see a cockroach
> creeping up the bedpost.

('Aftermath')

> Even in bed
> my self
> copulates with its own dry bones

leaving her body
pensile on the tide's crest
Nudity feels stripped
When the mind plays at
catching its own tail.

('Cerebral Love')

Arabian horses
snort around our bed
pawing into frosted holes.
...
Ask me not to act.
Deed is now my perdition.

('To A Younge Wife')

In the lines quoted above Shiv K. Kumar depicts the failure in love not in terms of betrayal by the beloved but in terms of fear psychosis and physical inadequacy on the part of the lover. This kind of attitude to man-woman relationship gives a new dimension to Kumar's poetry.

One important aspect of Kumar's love poetry is his projection of love and sex to the world of nature. Human love, perceived in terms of lanascape and nature makes an interesting study in Kumar's poetry. Poems like 'Kovalam Beach,' 'Mission Beach,' 'A Dark Mood,' and 'Fishermen' skilfully integrate human body and love with landscape and nature. In "Kovalam Beach," the theme of frustration in love and sex transferred to the elemental world of land and sea, finds an apt expression in the following lines :

Near the western horizon
below the descending tiers
of skin-head rocks
the vaginal creeks
lie open-thighed
in insatiable expectancy
while the sea's thrusts
break into surf
then recede

consummation thwarted
each time they
miss an ovary.

The waves reaching the shore is visualized in terms of human sexuality when the sea is taken as a male, mating with the shore, a female.

Again aspects of nature is visualised is sexual terms in a poem called, 'Fisherman,' where

...the sea convulses
to watch her secrets
laidout for marketing
on the sands.

In 'A Dark Mood' human love is perceived in terms of landscape and nature, when the poet says,

Not tonight —
not even if you creep foamfooted
into the bed
offering the salt-taste
of your flesh.

How can we exchange nudities to night
when the shells on the ocean's bed
are wailing for the dead?
...
A man should come to his woman whole —
not when the mind
is a perverted sunflower
turning face to darkness.

Kumar views love largely in terms of failure and holds the woman responsible for it. I am inclined to concur with Surjit S. Dulai when he makes a pertinent comment on this aspect in the following lines :

"Many poems in *Cobwebs* are about this tragedy, particularly in the form of the failures and frustrations in marriage caused mainly by the callous lovelessness of a female spouse. "Returning Home," and "Married Too Long" depict the unhappiness of a marriage gone bad. "My Mother's Lover," portrays a wife's infidelity. The best poems on the subject are the ones that show the destruction wreaked on the very manhood of the male partner by th woman's treacherous insensitivity. "To a Young Wife," "Back to Back," "Co-respondent," and "A Dark Mood" evoke the pathetic helplessness of a male whose very sexuality has been severely eroded by the circumstances of his situation" (JSAL 1992 : 20).

Subterfuges contains a number of love poems in the same mode as that of his earlier two volumes. In this volume (*i.e.*, *Subterfuges*) Kumar sees woman not an object of beauty but sees the ugliness, dirt and disease associated with life. It is a negative vision running counter to the romantic glorification of woman. The portrait of a Cabaret Dancer brings home not only the beauty of a woman but the ugliness hidden underneath as the Dancer kisses even the lepers 'on their flushed cheeks.' And as she kisses

> ...A frenzied moan curls up
> from Hades and all
> the animals are unleashed
> A scramble for a closer
> scrutiny of the deity.
> The star suddenly vanishes
> behind a laced veil —
> the temple doors are slammed

('Cabaret Dancer')

Like W.B. Yeats, Kumar speaks of sensuality as an act not unknown to gods for they are also engaged in physical act for pleasure. Thus, he writes :

> These stones have wings
> and darkness here flaps
> into phosphorescence.
> Washed by the semen
> of primeval gods
> playing under candid moonlight

they froze into sculpture
as the Sun broke in.

('The Sun Temple, Konarak')

Kumar's love poems are built on failures, betrayals and frustrations in life caused by the lack of constancy on the part of the 'woman.' Hence, his love poetry is associated with pain and suffering. To read his love poetry is to see the protagonist enacting his tragic play on the stage — it is to see him inside out.

In the formative years of his poetic career, Kumar like W.B. Yeats excels in his short lyrics. "Rickshaw-Wallah." "Duty Free," "Images," "I shall not gaze at the Moon Again," "Karma," "Sounds of Hunger," "The Face," "To a Young Wife," "Aftermath," "Epitaph on an Indian Politician," "Indian Women," "A Mango Vendor" and "My Co-respondent," are some of his best lyrics. In "Rickshaw Wallah," poverty as faced by countless millions of poor people is skilfully described. For a handful of coins, the Rickshaw Wallah pulls passengers, "On the cushioned seat behind" beyond the 'municipal precincts,' which is aptly compared with 'the mother-hen gagging her chicks, full throated cries/for a few grains of rice/their last supper.'

Shiv K. Kumar like other leading post-colonial Indian English poets such as Nissim Ezekiel, A.K. Ramanujan, Jayanta Mahapatra, R. Parthasarathy and a few others believes that our 'identity be symbolized anew.' The phase of nostalgic harking back to colonial past is over and Kumar has realised the world and felt it in his pulses. Poetry becomes a medium to interpret life and source of sustenance (an extension of Arnoldian vision of poetry that 'consoles and sustains us') for him.

If colonial poetry is about the coloniser, post-colonial poetry is in opposition to imperialism and an assertion of indigenous tradition and culture. Kumar also opposes the neo-colonialism of U.S.A. in a poem titled, "A Letter from New York." He makes two things clear in this poem — one, he takes a dig at the slavish attitude of the socalled Indian intellectuals, who think that the foreigners know best and everything foreign is better than indigenous things, and two, he affirms his indigenous belief and asserts his identity by refusing to be swayed away by the foreign flavour. Thus, he writes :

> Here I live in a garbage can
> and the pile grows bigger each week
> with the broken homes
> splintered all around.
>
> A black cat chases a shadow
> down the passageway :
> its whiskers presage another snowstrom.
> The white of the negro maid's eye balls
> is the only clean thing here,
> besides, of course, the quart gallon carton of milk
> squatting at my door.
> (Does Krishna, your boy servant,
> still clean his arse with milk
> before filling up the can
> with rain-water?)
>
> They wouldn't believe it here
> that the Ganges' water can work
> miracles like Lourde's,
> inspite of the cartloads of deadmen's ashes
> and bones and the pundits' shit —
> daily offerings to the Mother River!
>
> (A Letter from New York)

He asserts, 'but my soul is still my own' and refuses to fall in line with their way of life in New York. He asks :

> But the brown of my skin defies
> all bleachers,
> How long will the eclipse last?

This brings to one's mind R. Parthasarathy's *Rough Passage* in which he discards the foreign land (*i.e.*, England,) for it is not very different from that of ours' in its cleanliness and what is more, it is not broad enough to assimilate Indian sensibility into its fold and therefore, Parthasarathy decides to return home.

('Home Coming,' the third part of *Rough Passage* reinforces this idea). Kumar, like Parthasarathy resists the impact of foreign culture on him. Infact, one of the ingredients of post-colonial poetry is resistance to the former coloniser or present neo-coloniser.

In his specifically Indian poems like " Indian Women," "An Indian Mango Vendor," "Transcendental Meditation" and A. Hindu to his "Cow" Kumar reflects on the Indian situation as assertion of indigenous tradition and culture. The patience of Indian women waiting for their men's return is expressed through indigenous images in the following way :

> Patiently they sit
> like empty pitchers
> on the mouth of the village well ....
> waiting for their men's return
> till even the shadows
> roll up their contours
> and are gone
> beyond the hills
>
> (Indian Women)

And in between 'they guard their tattooed thighs' and resist 'the moisture in their eyes.' This is a typical image of Indian village women who are mostly devoted to their husbands. Constancy in love is a virtue for them. Waiting for their men is an act of faith that is fulfilled like the empty pitchers being filled with water in the village well, on their men's return. Waiting, infact becomes an act of affirmation of their love for their men.

In 'A Mango Vendor' a young youthful women sells mangoes, while attracting customers (including old men) by her beauty and charm. The poem is evocative of the bazar scene in our country. The sensual imagery successfully recreates the characters in their own situation. Thus, Kumar writes :

> She squats
> on the dust-broomed pavement
> behind a pyramid of mangoes

washed with her youth's milk
tinctured with the pink rose in her hair.
Through the slits
of her patched blouse
one bare shoulder
two white moons
pull all horses
off the track

('A Mango Vendor')

This image of 'the Mango Vendor' does not escape the eyes of an oldman, which tempt him to 'buy something.'

In "A Hindoo To His Cow," the cow is likened to mother and hence loved and respected by all Hindus. No matter how the cow is treated by others, to us, the Hindus she is the holy cow, as sacred as the Ganges. Thus, Kumar says,

Let them go beefing
around the coasts
from insects to mammals
from Hudson to Volga —
your mystique
only the Ganges will comprehend.

(A Hindoo To His Cow)

Like other post-colonial poets in India, African and Caribbean countries, Kumar has been busy with reviving the cultural identity that had been damaged by the colonial experience. I concur with Elleke Boehmer when she makes a pertinent point in this regard in the following lines :

"Indian, African and Caribbean nationalist writers focused on reconstituting from the position of their historical, racial or metaphysical difference a cultural identity which has been damaged by the colonial experience. The need was for roots, origins, founding myths and ancestors national foremothers and fathers : in short, for restorative history" (1995 : 185-186).

Kumar is alive to pain and suffering in life. He seems to have similar views on this aspect of life as that of T.S. Eliot and endorses the latter's observation 'people may change and smile but the agony abides.' That is why death becomes a major theme in Kumar's poetry. Poems like "An Encounter with Death," "And Death Shall Speak with Many Voices," and "My Mother's Death Anniversary," included in the first three volumes of Kumar's poetry amply demonstrate his preoccupation with death (This theme is further developed in his fourth book of verse, *Woodpeckers*). It is significant to note that Kumar began his poetic career with a poem on death (*i.e.*, 'An Encounter with Death') written after the death of his mother. Kumar's poetry owes its origin to his mother. In course of an interview with Saraswati Sabbu, Kumar speaks candidly about his mother and the origin of his poetry.

"As I said, being the youngest child, I had great affection and respect for my mother. If you find anything good in my poetry or in my fiction, it may have come to me from my mother. She had this sensitivity in her. Although not a highly educated woman, she had an artistic sensibility. I've always felt that she could have taken to writing. Though she thought in Hindi, she would read the *Gita* and daily newspaper. It was her vision of life and perceptiveness that educated me, ... In all my troubles and agony, it was my mother who comforted me. She helped me to understand myself better. When I lost her, I had come to terms with my innerself, I believe that the emotional trauma I suffered released all that poetic energy" (ILR : 7, October 1991).

In 'An Encounter with Death' Kumar not only describes the last moments of his mother's life but affirms his faith in the beliefs of the Hindus. He writes :

> ...my mother's hand was on her heart. Was she
> delicately poised on that thin 'borderline
> between existence and extinction, where
> eternity unfolds all her riddles? But
> before my arm could reach out to her,
> she slumped into oblivion.

> I was undone; in my feverish flush
> I heard the snapping of some mysterious
> bonds; it was now and not at my birth
> that the umbilical cord lay sundered.
>
> For thirteen days, say the Hindus, the departed
> soul hovers round its earthly habitat, and
> so for thirteen days, I have communed with the
> spirit — whenever a door-handle rattles, a
> nipping wind howls, the dog whines or the
> blue-bells clang, I feel her presence within me.
> Immanence is an attribute of God.

Death continues to haunt the poet. In "And Death Shall Speak with Many Voices," as G.S. Amur has rightly pointed out he "dramatizes a mood of calm acceptance of the fact of death :

> The flamingoes may now
> pick the unresonant bones.
> The ashes are waiting
> for the stray winds.

The poem works through a strong visual image, that of a body reduced to ashes by the flames of a pyre, reinforced by a series of auditory images :

> Soft mallet strokes
> on the navel,
> thrumming past the heart
> to seize the throat
> by its soprano chords
> and outshout its brazen denials
> till the membrane pops to silence.

In Indianness of such poems is evident not only in their unmistakbly Indian images like the Sandalwood Pyre, but in their attitude to death which is one of detached acceptance" (1979 : 129).

In "My Mother's Death Anniversary," the Poet seems to say that the time passes on as the pain continues to haunt our minds and the dead is remembered once a year by way of our performing the ritual. We move in time and death takes away the dead. What remains is only a sad memory of our dear ones who have been taken away by death. Thus, the poet says :

The clock-beat leaps
beyond the ECG's longitudes,
and far across the street
a pariah dog's wail
climbs up to the seedy moon.

Each year a day chooses me
to feed the dead.

Kumar writes more poems on death with objectivity after he has gained recognition as an Indian English Poet in the nineteen-eighties.

Like his contemporary post-colonial Indian English poets, Nissim Ezekiel, R. Parthasarathy and Kamala Das, Shiv K. Kumar too writes an autobiographical poem, "Broken Columns" in seven sections and later adds five more sections to it — the first version of the Poem is included in *Subterfuges* and the second version of it is published in *Woodpeckers*. 'Broken Columns' certainly has some elements of Kumar's life but it is not strictly an autobiographical poem or a confessional poem in the sense we take the confession poetry of a Robert Lowell or a Sylvia Plath. In course of two interviews — one with K. Venkatachari and another with Atma Ram — Kumar denies that this poem is autobiographical. He tells K. Venkatachari.

"It ('Broken Columns') only uses certain elements of my personal experience but it is not autobiography. Indeed, I would like to endorse what Robert Lowell once said about his own poetry! Most people, he remarked, forget that the socalled 'confessional' Poet often invents characters and situations under the pressure of imagination. Actuality tends to be restrictive, dull and amorphous — it is moulded into form only by the creative imagination" (JLA 1 : 3, 1981 : 17).

Again he reiterates this point in course of an interview with Atma Ram :

"I have often been labelled as a 'confessional' poet, and indeed in tone and structure my poetry may be called 'autobiographical.' But what most readers fail to comprehend is the fact that a poet often invents facts and experiences camouflaging them as 'real and authentic' — to achieve the reader's total participation. It's more a strategy of the imagination than a transcript of empirical reality" (Naik, 1979 : 127).

The poem begins when the poet was of four years of age and continues to develop with the growing of this child into manhood and maturity. The poem shows the conflict and tension between an individual who wants to grow with his innocence and simplicity on the one hand and the subterfuges of the society which tend to destroy the 'pre-lapsarian innocence' of the individual on the other. (A detailed analysis of the poem is given in Chapter III of this book).

One significant aspect of Kumar's poetry is that it transcends the limitations of an individual's life and achieves a kind of universality by speaking about the contemporary society and life, the world over. I am inclined to agree with Surjit S. Dulai when he says,

In the larger world beyond personal relationships, the "dead oyster-shells" of "Lear to Cordelia" expand into the waste land of the contemporary civilization, mostly associated, in Kumar, with the West. "On First Seeing a Skinflick," "At a Psychedelic Art Exhibition," " Fishermen," "Litterbox," "New Year's Eve," "Walking Down the Avenue of the Americas," "Memorial Service," and "Rush Hour" together provide a picture of the vulgarity, fragmentation, crassness, squalor, sterility, and the stress of modern life, especially in the West. The sea of "Fishermen" that stands for meaning as opposed to the banal, though necessary, purpose of the fishermen's work, also gives a peevish response.

> Sometimes she prevaricates
> ....
> she comes
> a little too soon
> to throw only slime-wrapped

rotund-bellied molluscs
at their loins.

"Refugees" describes the particular harshnessess suffered by those expelled from their homelands, a widely rampant contemporary phenomenon" (JSAL 1990 : 21).

In 'Refugees' the plight of refugees is brought out in realistic terms. The survival is in question. Thus, he writes :

From secure walls
to bare skies —
the snail's way
through the arid zones
of aching slime to the alien
lands of rude questionings
The Hiroshima faces, skull-thin,
eat shadows at noon.

Kumar is not blind to an Indian's predicament in America for it involves national identity. In 'A Letter From New York' quoted earlier in this chapter and "Walking Down the Avenue of the Americas," Kumar harks on this point of cultural alienation and identity crisis. While walking down the Avenue of the Americas, he feels alienated as he fails to identify himself with the natives. Being haunted by a sense of distrusts he writes :

Every passerby in polaroids
is my wife's seducer,
my child's kidnapper,
My reflection in every shop-window

is a portrait
of my ashes middle-age,
harassed bye pavements
hurling stones at me.

In a different context, Kumar writes how soothing it is to return home, where compromises are made for a better living. In "Returning Home," Kumar speaks of a warring couple who finally reconcile to each other. 'Home' is the place where one listens to the counsel of others and make amends. Thus, Kumar writes :

> Here in the open privacies
> the old gods counsel compromise.

This salutary conclusion reminds us of Nissim Eekiel's witty and prudent observation, "Home is where we have to gather grace." Kumar is in quest of prelapsarian innocence and to restore it no compromise is too high a price to pay. Kumar searches for the good in the evil and the good beyond the evil.

Kumar dramatizes his own failure or truimph, impotence or passion, love or hate, as 'the normal passionate, reasoning' man to reach an intense universality of meaning. To read Kumar's poetry is to watch an actor enacting his 'tragic play,' in all its facets — love, politics, sex, religion — on the stage, it is to know him inside out. His characters be it a poet laureate, a politician, a prostitute, a cabaret dancer a co-respondent a rickshaw-walla — all come alive in their own situations. That is why Kumar's world is warm, palpable and dynamic, his characters are vividly present and recognizable in terms of 'chief intensity' as the poet himself. Aboveall, his early poetry is like a bud that blossoms into a beautiful flower in his later poetry. With the first three volumes of his poetry Kumar has not only made a beginning but announced his triumphant arriving.

WORKS CITED

Amur, G.S. "Poetry as Subterfuge : An Introduction to Shiv K. Kumar's Poetry." *Aspects of Indian Writing in English*. Ed. M.K. Naik, Madras : MacMillan, 1979.

Boehmer, Elleke. *Colonial and Postcolonial Literature*. New York : Oxford University Press, 1995.

Dulai, Surjit S. "Shiv K. Kumar's Writing." *Journal of South Asian Literature* 25 : 2 (Summer, Fall 1990) : 9-48.

Ram, Atma. "Interview with Shiv K. Kumar," Quoted. *Aspects of Indian Writing in English*. Ed. M.K. Naik, Madras : MacMillan, 1979.

Sabbu, Saraswasti. "Shiv K. Kumar : An Interview." *Indian Literary Review* : 7 October 1991. Rep. JSAL 25 : 2, 1990 : 227-228.

Venkatachari, K. "Interview with Shiv K. Kumar." *Journal of Literature and Aesthetics* 1 : 3, (June 1981) : 15-22.

3

The Attainment

Shiv K. Kumar published his fourth book of verse, *Woodpeckers* in 1979. Death is the overwhelming theme in this well knit and worked out book, which contains twentyfive poems. This theme is a continuation of his earlier preoccupation with death (It is an irony of fate that Kumar's first poem is written on the death of his mother and titled "An Encounter with Death") and a corrollary to his themes of pain and suffering. Apart from this theme, there are poems on human love, an autobiographical poem, 'Broken Columns' and a few topical poems. With this volume Kumar has discovered his voice and mastered the art of writing poetry effectively.

Let me begin with the first poem of the book, 'Broken Columns,' which is made longer with the addition of five long sections to its earlier version published in *Subterfuges*. It reminds us of Ezekiel's "Background, Casually," Kamala Das's "An Introduction," and R. Parthasarathy's Rough Passage and is written in the confessional mode. It covers a long period of Kumar' life — from the age of four through puberty, trip to England for higher study, to an unhappy marriage and the resultant divorce. The dovetailing of images and the authorial comments make this autobiographical poem both interesting and enjoyable. The opening lines of the poem make he poet's attitude towards his parents crystal clear. It is his love for his mother and emotional attachment to her that bring out the 'poet' in the man into the open. Father takes a back seat. Thus, he writes :

You're now four,
you may drink up
all the glaciers
nibble at raw pebbles
but not suck away.'
Father's barb fell blunted
against Mother's Smile

(Broken Columns I)

Father's advice and attitude to life and above all, his philosophy was beyond the comprehension of a boy of seven. The killing of goats and the butcher's cruel act of separating 'heads intestines, thighs and shoulders' disturbs the poet's father, who explodes :

"Karma will run its cycle when these
maimed animals rise
to gobble down these shoppers!

(Section II)

If butcher's cruelty hurts a child of seven years of age, 'a beggar's sunken belly' across the pavement brings to his mind the poverty of India in unmistakable terms. At the advent of puberty, the boy gets disturbed both at school and in the evening prayer at home. As Kumar puts it :

At ten I play hide and seek
down the school-lane in a shop
stacked with teak and deodar
and suddenly Sheila's chequered
skirt blows into life

(Section III)

In the evening when all the members of the family begin their prayer with chants from the Gita, the adolecent boy visualises the girl in the following way :

A puff of deodar rustles
through a girl's skirt
and two tender legs
gyrate the air into fuzzy yearnings.

(Section IV)

As the poetic persona grows in years, at fourteen he encounters in the history classroom the ruins of the Mughal Empire and sees the nakedness of British imperialism — both political and cultural. Hence, Indians realise the waste and lament :

> We pant on the dunes
> of the relentless Sahara.
>
> (Section V)

The poem moves first in time and the poet describes the passion in life at twenty. The Biblical image befits the situation as the passion in him grows and demands consumption. Kumar's choice of words is commendable.

> At twenty
> I see a girl's bodice shimmer
> in the water's eye. I am
> the Adam who has just founded
> a new city
> named all its streets.
>
> (Section VI)

The physical passion reigns supreme as the first-love making underlines 'no commitment to the stars, she knew/only a beetle's mating drone.' This love relationship needs a legal sanction — we may say using Edward Said's terminology, the 'filiation' needs 'affiliation' — and therefore, the father sniffing 'danger in scraps/of scented pink paper/ blown from my pockets' sends the son to the temple priest for advice. The undertone of irony is unmistakable. Kumar writes :

> In the meditation-room
> of the Shiva temple
> the high priest communes with Brahma
> wrapped in saffron loin-cloth
> he lets his long, grey hair
> cascade down to life's quiddity
> As he bekons me into the dark chamber
> I pull myself out of the earth's orbit
> into blank space.
> ....

But as I emerge from the netherworld
an aroma of deodar wells up
and a cluster of mynas hurls
defiance at the truth.

(Section VII)

Next section of the poem is about the protagonist's stay at Cambridge and another love affair there — 'young Siddhartha swigs off/the champagned nipples.' But there is a harking back to the past in the letter to the mother. There is also a realisation that absolute freedom could be destructive. Thus, the poet writes :

'Freedom is the demon
that devours its own brood.'

Love at Cambridge became painful for the protagonist, because it turned out to be unrequited and unsuccessful. Hence, the protagonist returned home and searched for a new bride. The bitterness for the failure in love at Cambridge is conveyed to us in the imagery of a bird which stretches its wing too much and comes to grief in the end.

The bird that stretches its wing
beyond the water's brink
often lands on some insidious rock
Even the sky has its enemies —

(Section X)

But the marriage, turns out to be a disastrous one resulting in a divorce. 'The Seven Circles round the holy fire' proved to be an exercise in futility for the woman had different perceptions of life. The poet uses animal and serpent imagery to bring home the nature of the incompatible woman.

How could a Zebra be yoked to carry
cabbages to the market place?....
The cobra eye held me
whichever way I turned;
venom oozed from the earth
to blight all roots.

(Section XII)

The poem ends with divorce and separation but the agony abides, as the protagonist says I loved you most when I forsook you.' The autobiographical note is unmistakable.

In *Woodpeckers* Kumar is 'possesed by death' and like John Webster 'saw skull beneath the skin.' He is deeply pained to find that 'resilience is not for everybody/some perish in the womb/before sunrise.' The theme of death, already introduced in his early poetry is now carried further with new insight and experience. "Crematorium in Adikmet, Hyderabad" describes the last rites performed by Hindus and the poet takes a dig at the undesirable things that happen during such solemn function. The beggars, the vultures and the priest vitiate the atmosphere of performing the last rites and the relatives of the dead get disgusted at the commercial attitude of the priests and the pestering of the beggars. With a note of disgust and irony the poet works out the poem and spares none who is responsible for lowering the dignity of the funeral ceremony. This is how the poem begins :

> Incessant din of beggars
> and chants.
> A skull rolls out of a drainhole.
> Perched on the wall a vulture cogitates
> upon human avidity — flesh offered
> to the flames, bones and ashes
> to the Ganges. No leavings
> for the living.

The assonance and homophony in the last two lines quoted above are poignant for they explain the futility of human condition. And the crematorium is the place that wipes out human existence and all come here sooner or later. No one can evade it. Thus, the poet writes :

> Here the earth replenishes itself —
> wipes out a name to welcome
> a fresh arrival.

Kumar describes death and burial at the Ghats of Banaras. Death leaves none — 'a child' or 'a young courtesan' all meet the same fate. All the dead bodies thrown to the river amidst the 'priest's chant' lose their existence and get extinct in the deep water. Thus, the poet writes :

> On the western ghat
> a glassy-eyed crocodile dips
> into sacrosanct waters
> to cleanse its scales —
> its belly mirroring
> all faces of death.
>
> ('At the Ghats of Banaras')

"A Dead Bird on an Electric Pole" tells us about the pervasive nature of death. Death leaves no one — bird or animal, saint or sinner. Kumar's apt observation, 'the invisible always hurts more,' has a universal ring about it. A blow from the invisible is far more painful than the wound inflicted on us by some known sources. Electricity does not distinguish between good or bad, innocent or wicked. Thus, Kumar writes :

> The electric chair is neutral
> to bird, assassin and saint.

But Kumar is not a pessimist. He accepts death as it comes to people or birds. He does not wish to run away. On the contrary he takes a dig at the rituals associated with death. Surjit S. Dulai makes an interesting comment on Kumar's poems on death in the following lines :

> A new development in Kumar's poetry as evidenced in *Woodpeckers* is strong preoccupation with death. Dealth, a recurring subject earlier, dominates the new poems in the collection. Some poems focus on death directly. In "Crematorium in Adikmet, Hyderabad," at the cremation of his father, the speaker watches death with an unsentimental, ironic gaze. A "vulture cogitates" to see "No leavings/for the living." Death is an eternal fact of existence. "Here the earth replenishes itself...." "At the Ghats of Banaras" shows that death knows

no distinction between youth ("a child's lissom body" and age, the noble and the ignoble ("warm ashes of a young courtesan"), animal (a "pet dog") and human. Against this backdrop, the poem depicts the futility of religious rituals and the cynicism of the worldly towards the dead like the "glassy-eyed crocodile," "its belly mirroring/all faces of death." "Thanksgiving" brings out the cruel irony of a turkey's slaughter for the occasion. The poem captures vividly the bird's flamboyant handsomeness, evokes the picture of "a hen with five chicks," thus, portraying them together touchingly as living creatures. The ritual prayer of thanksgiving degrades the killing of the bird to worse than its death. The most beautiful poem on death is "A Dead Bird on an Electric Pole." The dead bird is described with concrete sharpness. The immutable hardness of death is brought home with full force. Yet there are intimations of an infinite reality beyond horizons, beyond physical death. And within the finite, death is still surrounded by life.

> Around the scaffold a thrush
> is looping the loop —
> its throat jammed in a mute requiem.

Many more poems than the ones dealing directly with death are charged with a death-like feeling rather than addressing death literally. It is as if the poet were up against life's finite limitations, sensing its dead-end quality. Whatever its cause — middle age, growing awareness of life's inevitable end, some psychological or physical trauma — the feeling is unmistakable. It appears in poem after poem — as in "Flower-pot in My Study" ("Stirrings in a painted skull"), "Mango Grove,"

> "Above my head clusters of virgin breasts
> of peasant women
> kneeling over graves...."

and "School Children During Lunch Break,"

> The sky drops pollens
> over the dead.
> The earth smooths its creases."

(JSAL : 25 : 2 : 26-27)

The ruin of monuments caused by the onslaughts of nature pains Kumar and he expresses his sense of disappointment over the decline of Tajmahal's beauty. He writes :

> Fissures in its rectum —
> now a renovator's nightmare.
> How long can it withstand
> the riverbed's lethal teeth?
>
> ('The Taj')

Decay and death cause anguish in the heart of the Poet and he writes with insight into human nature. Birje-Patil makes an interesting observation on this point.

"To seek unity among all living things through death the leveller with a lightness of touch is part of Kumar's achievements in *Woodpeckers*. The poem where death does not occur or where it rumbles distantly like an echo do not, as in the earlier volumes, terminate on academic resolution. Some of them bewitch by their daring simplicity" (Kulshrestha 1980 : 242).

> Like a teddy-bear's button-eyes
> its berries dazzle
> with their precocious stare.
>
> (Flower-Pot in my Study)

In 'To an Unborn Child' one hears a distant echo of Louis MacNeice's poem, 'Prayer Before Birth.' Kumar wants to warn the unborn child against the harsh realities of the world. The negative attitude springs from Kumar's anguish, for he has felt the pinch of life at the hands of friends and relatives alike. But Kumar is not a pessimist. Inspite of all odds he wants the child to be born. Thus, he writes :

> I'm sorry you'll inherit
> this subfusc earth
> we've just move into this limbo
> whose walls are papered with unpaid bills
> And on each day of reckoning
> I play truant while your mother
> feigns hysteria

come on in —
we're waiting.

Pain and suffering in life continue to worry the poet right from the beginning of his poetic career. His poetry is a vertible apotheosis of tragic affirmation. He feels that suffering is inevitable and accepts life as it comes. As he put it :

I never broke any law
of the god's stern eye.
Yet this fulvous moisture
On my palm
my body drenched in cold sweat —
in pain.

(Rain)

In "Midnight Musings" the same theme is reinforced and the poet says it with a note of anguish and despair.

The moment of despair
has no age
no discretion
At fifty-two I see eucalyptus
thighs waiting to be hustled
by a mere sunset.

Acceptance of pangs of life, pain and suffering leads to a kind of indifference. It inspires the poet to live alone without having attachment for anything. In "Detachment" he says,

Let the waters carry away the ashes
swiftly past the antique bridge
not swing back to smudge
the rock that has known many a corpse.

('Detachment')

Wit and humour are an integral part of Kumar's life as well as poetry. The birth of a son and the attachment to his mother resulting in the father's loss of privacy and monopoly with her is skilfully worked out in a poem called 'My Son.' The father asks the son about the latter's birth in the following way :

Were you with us even then
like the third traveller
on the road to Emmaus —
seeing, hearing everything?

After nine harvest moons
one afternoon
you barged in knocking the front
door off its hinges
to grab my woman
nibble toothlessly at her moist nipples.

Even impostors have some graces
but you arrive with the assurance
of a state warrant
and I surrender willingly
to you —
my compeer.

In "Lord Venkateswara's Temple" the poet takes a dig at the hypocrisy in the society. Thus, he writes :

Oppressed by omniscience
the Lord smiles at daily somersaults—
why should repentance endure
beyond sunset?

The implicit irony makes Kumar's poetry lovable and worth-enjoying. Thus, he writes :

Once, so goes the legend,
a young fisherwoman in rags
came to the Lord straight
from her son's burial —
lay prostrate at the shrine's threshold
but asked for no boon
not even peace for her son's soul.

Behind all kinds of failures in life and the threat of death, there lies the frustration resulting out of a wife's desertion and divorce and Kumar returns to this theme again and again. In otherwords this is a Freudian slip in Kumar's poetry. Here are two examples :

I know where my wife's secrets
lie sealed. Each night I hear
the same tattoo in my skull's chamber.

('Insomnia')

I rise from my bed
in search of movement
in the grass
but nothing stirs
not even my wife deserting.

('Autumn')

Shiv K. Kumar's Central Sahitya Akademi Award Winning book of verse, *Trapfalls in the Sky* contains three sections : "On Native Grounds," "Under Alien Skies" and 'Genesis.' The theme of landscape and national identity makes a rewarding study in Kumar's poetry and *Trapfalls in the Sky* bears testimony to it. The poems are very simple at the surface level but at the deep structure level, they make a difficult reading. Kumar wrote a number of topical poems in the first section ('On Native Grounds') of *Trapfalls in the Sky.* The poem called, "An Indian Mother's Advice to her Daughter Before Marriage' is a typical example of how Indian mothers tender advice to their daughters to get in on in married life.

Don't ever argue
at the moment of surrender
for the end is ineluctable.
...
But take time unfolding yourself.
Let him first burn
awhile on the hot sand
for this is also the moment of claiming
not giving in only.

Like Ezekiel, Kumar is against mechanical performance of rituals. He is in favour of the subversion of tradition and rituals and, therefore, irony becomes a favourite mode in his poetry.

Since Ganga can't cleanse us, we need to cleanse it to get rid of water pollution. Thus, he writes :

> May be if someone could dismantle all scaffoldings
> along the mother river's waistline
> and ask the dead to seek immersion
> in other confluences,
> the little fish will then bleach these waters
> for the sun's lasers to probe her limpid groin.
>
> The moon will recapture in the river's mirrors
> the sharp lineaments of her own face
> flushed like a bride's
> as she walks into the nuptial chamber
> holding a lone candle
> to be snuffed out
> into the Bay's eternity.

('Cleansing Ganga')

As a post-colonial poet, Kumar makes an attempt to write authentically about contemporary reality. The picture of the capital city of India (*i.e.*, Delhi) is revived in a poem called "O'Delhi." To read the poem is to dive deep into this city and it is to see it inside out. Kumar recalls his harrowing days when he landed in Delhi as a refugee. In a 'frigid morning' when Kumar landed in Delhi, it received him with open arms.

> You were then my santa Claus who pulled down
> the moon for me, studded with stars in her gridle
> and the ghazals of Ghalib and Zauq on her lips.

But this Delhi is no more. The poet, who like Adam inherited 'a new garden' asks Delhi : 'what have you done to yourself?' And then makes a prophesy :

> I prophesy that you too will fall
> like Nineveh and Babylon
> and no new Indraprastha will rise
> from your, barren ashes.

The delay in getting justice and the inherent drawback in our judiciary come under scrutiny in a poem titled "Tis Hazari Courts, Delhi." Kumar like Ezekiel is unsparing in his criticism of a system that denies the people from getting justice. Thus, he writes :

> From the murky corridors of this labyrinths
> there's no escape. Since time began
> I've watched the victims enter from the eastern
> gate — and then only the smoke exits
> from the other end.

And again using Shakespearean model 'Poet, Lover and Lunatic,' Kumar says about the fate of 'lover, the cancer patient and the petitioner' :

> It's the long wait that kills
> the lover, the cancer-patient
> and the petitioner.
>
> ("Tis Hazari Courts, Delhi")

In another poem called 'Refugees,' Kumar reflects on the miserable condition of the refugees and brings home their plight in the changing situation.

> Blinkered like yoked bulls,
> burdened with ancestral memories,
> they trudge on, counting the milestones
> which look like maimed tombstones
> while the time's womb holds out
> only a still-born.
>
> ('Refugees')

The plight of the Eunuchs is depicted in a poem called 'Eunuchs' in a similar manner as Mahesh Dattani later on does in his *Collected Plays*. Eunuchs who bring luck to others on some occasions, themselves remain cursed. That is the irony of their lives. Kumar writes :

> A whisper in the air, a cloudburst,
> a star dislodged from the sky's hem, or
> a squint in the storm's eye

may send them off tripping
to a door that has been blessed —
a wedding anniversary,
a son's thread ceremony
even a cow's first delivery.
....
Between their cymbal — palms, the stray winds
break into song
that brings you blessings from their gods
who themselves died boonless.

('Eunuchs')

The title poem 'Trapfalls in the Sky' gives an assertion of Kumar's insight into life. Though it seems to be cynical, it is not so. Kumar visualises a world and sees into life :

Now that the candle is sinking
on its elephantiasis foot
of sprawling wax, I see in the sky
only trapfalls into which have vanished
all my liquid asserts

The second section of the poem is about East-West encounter. S.S. Dulai makes a pertinent comment on this in the following lines :

The West is a deep and vital influence in the shaping of Kumar's sensibility. Having intermittently lived for years, as a student or a teacher, in England, the U.S.A., and Australia, Kumar has had a close lifelong contact with the western civilization. This added to over two hundred years of western influence on Indian culture itself gives Kumar's writing its characteristic significance. His work reflects a perennial interaction between what he appears to see as the respective values of the Indian and the Western cultures. Almost constantly, his work is held in a tension between opposite modes of thought and behaviour associated, generally and in Kumar, with the two cultures. On the one hand are the primarily empirical thinking bordening on agnosticism and a lax sexual behaviour commonly perceived as western in origin. On the other hand are the primacy of intuition, faith, restraint and endurance usually considered the typical Eastern values. In his treatment of life in the West, Kumar presents a generally unflattering picture of it. His eye alights mainly on the outer squalor and harshness and an inner loneliness of the spirit that confront him as striking facts of human existence on both sides of the Atlantic despite material affluence. "Litterbox," "Walking Down the Avenue of the Americas," and "A Letter from New York" portray in scathing terms the deprivation and the ugliness that Kumar sees and the suffocation of the soul that he experiences in New York. Here one lives in an "inverted manhole" or "a garbage can, "with broken homes/ splintered all around." "The white of the black maid's eyeballs/is the only clean thing here...." One works for a boss whose grin shows "all the cavities/of his soul." There are tell-tale signs of racial discrimination. There "are no beggars," "cripples," or "lepers," asking for aims, "only eyes, eyes, eyes/ staring at lamp-posts" (1990 : 32-33).

Kumar has all the three qualities 'abundance, variety and complete competence' for which Eliot praises Tennyson and what is more, he has insight into human sexuality. When he writes frequently about love and sex, he is misunderstood by the critics but what most of the learned critics fail to see is Kumar's attitude to sex — he is not advocating the cause of sex or glorifying it, on the contrary debunking it. In a poem titled, "Shakespeare Seminar : Fall 1981," Kumar debunks a Professor who wants to spend his week-end with a lady student and borrowing the images from Othello, he writes :

> Lie with her! Lie on her!
> Noses, ears and lips!
> Is this an epilogue to a goatish week-end?
> So that's why Sheila never turns in her paper
> on time. But should I feel jaundiced
> if the cuckoo mates under a cornice
> in a grocery store, above the frozen meats —
> legs, thighs and breasts?

A stranger lying for a young female Jogger comes in for severe criticism in a Poem titled, "A Young Female Jogger." Kumar says :

> But the doves of your breasts
> leaving a trail of eau de jasmine
> and sweat give you away as some Jane,
> Susan or Nancy — or another Diana
> charged to outfly the fawn
>
> If hips, thighs and calves sway to
> same rhythm, it must be a sort of
> love-play that knows how to leap across
> a pot-hole in the side-walk, an arc of the sky
> and also swing in bed.
>
> I wonder who awaits you at the track's end.
> Will he mate you steel upon flint
> or just go down on his knees
> for a spurt of nectar
> from your navel?

Kumar like R. Parthasarathy longs to return home. He sees the life in the west and thinks of his own country and returns home. It is often said that one may take a person outside the country but not the country out of his/her mind. Kumar amply proves this point in "Heathrow Airport : Immigration Checkpost" and 'A Reminiscence.'

> You'll break through the sound
> barrier only if your dart hits
> the god's eye. Otherwise, the silver
> trawlers flying the royal ensign may
> whirl you back to your genesis.
>
> ("Heathrow Airport : Immigration Checkpost")
>
> Done with cambridge, I let a train
> disgorge me at Liverpool street,
> East End. Blindfolded by the late autumn
> smog, the sun gropes for an exit.
>
> ("A Reminiscence")

Kumar depicts authentically the East-West relationship and is never prejudiced against the one or the other. The third section 'Genesis' examines the origin of the creation of the world. Here the Poet makes a synthesis of the Eastern and the Western view of the creation of this world. I am inclined to concur with Surjit S. Dulai on the following point :

"Elements of both Western and Indian origin, thus combine in Kumar's poetry to provide an ecumenical duality of distinctions between sacred and profane, sublime and mean, good and bad in strictly human terms. He applies these distinctions evenly across his experience, Indian or Western. The genesis of his sensibility and the scope of his subject matter alike make him a writer of worldwide importance. Kumar's wide perspective on the world grows still wider — it acquires cosmic proportions in 'Genesis,' the last section of Trapfalls. In this poem, the heritage of Biblical, Islamic, and Hindu mythologies and the literary legacies of Milton, Goethe, love poetry in Sanskrit, Persian and Urdu-Hafiz, Ghalib, and Iqbal — blend into one in Kumar's sensibility to create quintessential images of man and woman and what makes human life human. Although extraterrestrial beings — God and Satan — are there, their presence is but a backdrop to the central fact of human existence, its vast significances rippling towards infinity" (1990 : 34).

God created man out of dust and as He 'breathed into his nostrils the breath of life,' man 'became a living soul.' He gives reasons behind the Creation in the following manner :

> It was the urge to commune
> with a sentient being —
> not just cattle, fish and flora —
> that I breathed into this lump of clay,
> moulded in my own likeness.
>
> ('Birth of Adam')

And Adam in his sleep dreams of a woman, to be called Eve :

> a bosom with two moons,
> shoulders like mute doves,

lips like two petals peeled off a gold cup,
eyes that spellbind a pansy —
and in her gait the swing of a dancing peacock.
('Birth of Eve')

And the irony of the situation is that Adam never imagined that someday this Eve 'may lead him into disheritance.' Satan in the form of the serpent tempts Eve to eat the fruit of the forbidden fruit and Eve gave in. Adam followed the suit to express his solidarity with her. Adam braved the punishment and said :

that to have dominion over my woman
during day, I must give in after dusk
that a curse may turn into a boon
denial into affirmation....
And if to know is to die,
why not perish together?
('Adam to Eve')

Eve reassures Adam of her love for him and does not regret the fall.

Shall I regret letting a stranger
hiss into my ears? I was always there
for you to decode my body, hear my
throat's birdsong. But we'd just lie
together alongside, like two sundered
boughs of the same tree.

And now this wanton urge
to bite the apples
off each other's breasts...
What beast is now crying out within me
for redemption?
('Eve to Adam')

Kumar imagines the fall out of the World's creation and feels for a moment that perhaps God is remorseful for the fall of man. Kumar's wistful thinking puts the following lines into God's mouth :

But now that they're gone
I feel forsaken too.
Down there, I see the Serpent's ravage
littered all around — the sere leaf
the cloven seed, the moth smothered
between an octopus's claws,
the locust sucking blood off a beanstalk's
neck — and the apple, now tainted at the core,
like a deadly mole.

["After the Departure of Adam and Eve from Eden" (God's Monologue)]

Trapfalls in the Sky justifies its title in the last section of the book 'Genesis' and looks forward to a new kind of poetry in the form of man's struggle for existence and encounter with reality in Kumar's next book of poems, *Woolgathering* (1998).

Woolgathering contains sixty poems on various themes such as love, death, contemporary reality, landscape, seasons and a few poems about family. The thematic range is wider than all his earlier poetry volumes and not only that, the perception of new reality makes the reasonance of Kumar's poetic voice distinct and unmistakable. Let us begin with Kumar's love poems. Human love is the central theme of his poetry. Frustration in love and betrayal by friends are major preoccupations in this book. Kumar like English metaphysical poets depicts various moods of love with insight and precision.

In 'Bedroom' Kumar tells us about a couple who, though lie 'together in bed' are distanced from each other by misunderstanding and 'daily wrangles.' It is not the closeness of the bodies but the minds that brings the couple together. Love is in the mind not in the body, Kumar seems to say.

If time and space lend perspective
to the mind, we should have learnt
to shift the word from its resonance.

To change a bed's locus-standi
each autumn

may not retrieve anything
when the mind is still shadowed by the bat's wings.
(Woolgathering : 45)

"Twenty-fifth Wedding Anniversary" generalises the problem that bedevils wife-husband relationship in 'Bedroom.' Kumar debunks hypocrisy in no uncertain terms. The hide and seek played by the wife and the husband disturbs the poet. The innocence is drowned in double-dealing and pretention. The misunderstanding between the wife and the husband is deep rooted and therefore, there is no love between them — only suspicion and distrust. Thus, the poet employs a gruesome image to describe their relationship in the following lines :

Your impulsion to needle
each word I spoke
as if it were some brown worm squirming.

The guests pretending happiness in married life wish the hosts 'many returns of the day' and therefore, the poet ridicules such people in no uncertain terms. He says,

...they have started to pour in,
each wearing his own anniversary on his painted face
poised to wish us many returns of the day —
or the night of eternal discord?
('Twenty-fifth Wedding Anniversary')

The imagery in his love poems is highly innovative, learned and original. Love and sex are depicted with consummate skill and the ideas are successfully conveyed through the imagery. Infact, in Kumar's poetry, particularly in his love poetry the image is the idea and therefore, the hints and guesses 'whisper results.' Thus, he writes :

Each icon of love speaks
its own language —
husky cooing in a thistle —
down bed, eyes that seek the meaning
of pollen wafting from one blue-bell
to another — and fingers that weave

occult patterns around brown nipples,
till even stone melts into benediction.

('Rape')

Likening the final assult in sex act to 'legs pinioned like a fowl's/before it is traded off' and the arousal of sex to 'moon tide' and the post-sex act to 'the moon hiding/behind a fugitive cloud/and the stars sniggering,' is to create innovative images to judge human love and sex in terms of the movement of the stellar bodies. In another poem called, 'The Ring' the comparison between talisman (*i.e.*, the Ring) and lie, desire and 'an abandoned mackerel' speaks volumes for Kumar's insight into image making. This is how the comparison has been brought out in the following lines :

It's my talisman against the wind's
whispering campaign.
Grown, smoother and wider
like a lie, it can now let
any questioning glide through.
....
The games are done only when the knuckles
shrivel up, the nails show
their white flags for truce
and desire lies gasping on the sand
like a mackerel abandoned
by the receding combers.

('The Ring')

Sleeplessness caused by one's wife's infidelity is brought out in a subtle way in a poem called 'Insomnia.' Failure in love and distrust in marriage are recurrent themes in Kumar's poetry. As he puts it :

I have counted all the stars
over my terrace. The steel bars in my
neighbour's balcony are twenty one
and three suburban freight trains rumble past
the rail-crossing between two and four.

Darkness now snaps at the seams.
A hymn floats across the sky
like a bird's warble....
— the milkman's bottle
jingles at my door step.

I must walk through the day's fire
to let another moon demolish me.

('Insomnia')

Unhappy conjugal life haunts the poet without end and in his poetry one discerns the groundswell of frustration in love in one's life due to the infidelity of the woman. I concur with Surjit S Dulai when he says :

"Conjugal unhappiness continues to be a frequent theme of Kumar's in this collection. He seems to see disharmony in marriage as a rampant phenomenon in the modern world. All the guests in "Twenty-fifth Wedding Anniversary," are wearing a mask of happiness in marriage and wishing the hosts "many returns of the day," while they know fully well the truth is otherwise. If possibilities of 'extra-marital romance arise, they are smothered by the hovering ghosts of wedded partners ('Thou Shalt Not Commit' and 'Ghosts'). 'I am a Vegetarian' is a lighthearted picture of a husband thinking about the consequences of weakness — 'a lamb's liver, a chicken's breast' — in his relationship with his 'shrewish wife.' Most poems about marriage are about a man's unhappiness caused by a woman's heartlessness. But the most moving poem on the subject, 'First Night — After a Doweried Wedding,' describes the feelings of a bride, victim of the common Indian customs of arranged marriage, a custom that pays scant regard to the bride's feelings, making marriage synonymous with death" (JSAL 1990 : 37).

If love takes a substantial part of Kumar's Poetry, death as a theme is also given a prominent place in it. Since pain and suffering are integral part of life, death and resurrection are recurrent themes in this book of verse (*i.e.*, *Woolgathering*). In "The Death of my Father," the poet expresses a personal sorrow, which gets impersonalised and objectified in the last stanza of the poem. The sorrow for not being able to attend the father's funeral makes him feel nostalgic about the past. Thus, he writes :

> Since I arrived here a day after the flames
> had already eaten you away
> I could commune only with your last remains.
> ....
> and I'll be ambushed by memories of my childhood —
> how you'd scold a boy of five
> for emerging from his shower,
> draped only in his nudity, as though to show
> that we shared something (besides our fierce dissents)
> that had been denied to mother and my sisters.

The personal loss is objectified as the poet tries to universalize this kind of emotion on the part of the protagonist. Thus, the poetic persona becomes anyman who mourns the death of his father. As Kumar puts it :

> Now I feel like a child
> playing marbles down a blind lane
> with a ghost, whose hands weave in the air
> patterns of a familiar sound.

In "Crematorium of Adikmet, Hyderabad," the poet describes how creamation has become a mere ritual, when priests take it as a kind of business ('The Priest chants louder/for a generous tip'). And the ritual continues. In the words of the poet,

> Here the earth replenishes itself —
> wipes out a name to welcome
> a fresh arrival.

Death is depicted as inevitable in some of Kumar's poems. The idea is to accept it as one accepts life. Once that is realized, death will cease to be terrible and dreadful.

Kumar wrote a number of poems on man's predicament in this harsh world and the first person narrative gives a kind of authenticity to these poems. Right from the beginning of his poetic career, Kumar has been preoccupied with human suffering and that is why, in his poetry there is a constant search for innocence and concern for the well being of individual human being. Poems like "Shadow Lines," "Sleep Walking," "Blackout" and "On Moving into a Complex of Apartments" reflect the condition of an individual in different situations. The uncertainty of the future looms large in the face of a person as the fate is governed by celestial bodies. Thus, he writes :

> My morning mirror shows a configuration
> of shadow lines as though the crisscrosses
> on my palms have surfaced here,
> presaging disasters.
>
> ("Shadow Lines")

> ...for compulsions have their own logic
> Horoscopes are never governed
> by terrestrial laws
>
> ('On Moving into a Complex of Apartments')

If Postcoloniality, which is currently in fashion, emphasizes a contemporary state, Kumar like his contemporaries, Nissim Ezekiel, Jayanta Mahapatra and A.K. Ramanujan is a Postcolonial poet par excellence. Kumar writes a number of topical poems (*i.e.*, Poems of contemporary interest). In two poems, 'I Say it on Oath, Your Lordship' and "Farewell to Tis Hazari Courts, Delhi," Kumar reflects on the Court scene. In the first poem the protagonist is pleading for his divorce from a nagging wife in a tone marked by anguish and disgust. The imagery employed is evocative and highly suggestive. Kumar writes :

> Speaking out one's mind in an open court
> is always an embarrassment
> like the wedding — kiss,
> under the priest's direction
> so may I use my own language, please,
> which speaks more through vehicle
> than tenor?
>
> I was always subjected to the terrors
> of her scimitar-tongue, which hurt me

like a surgeon, doing the stitches
without anaesthesia
.....
Even on our anniversaries,
if I ever let my desire speak
the body's language as a gesture,
She immediately receded
into the other hemisphere
where the moon hibernates and the sun
blazes its copper to dry even the spittle.
....
....Your lordship,
how I have withstood these assaults
on my mind's fragile fortress
But now I pray that this siege be lifted....

("I Say it an Oath, Your Lordship")

Kumar is upagainst hypocrisy, falsehood and double dealing. His idea of morality is linked with simplicity, honesty and innocence. In course of an interview with Indian Literary Review representative, Saraswati Sabbu, April 1989, reproduced in Journal of South Asian Literature 25 : 2 (Summer, Fall- 1990), on being asked about is adea of morality he says,

"Morality? You ask me a very significant question. Dedication and simplicity of the self are important. That is why I satirize urbanized modes of perception. I come down heavily on people living in big towns, the hypocrisy linked to the social system. I debunk the judiciary in my poem on Tis Hazari Courts. What about falsehood, hypocrisy, religion and pure orthodoxy? A simple person, who does his work right, is to me a little god; an uncomplicated human being. The woman in my poem "A Woman Labourer, Breast-feeding her Child, during Lunch-break" just carries bricks. She is not interested in anything else. Yet, to me she is the Madonna herself. Another poem on Mother Teresa — it's not what you do for yourself. So, I have a system of values. This is my morality" (JSAL : 234).

Kumar's "Farewell to Tis Hazari Courts, Delhi," a sequel to his earlier poem, "Tis Hazari Courts, Delhi" (included in *Trapfalls in the Sky*) reminds us of Nissim Ezekiel's poem, "Undertrial Prisoners" in which the latter underlines the lacunae in the judiciary system.

Kumar's topical poems reflect not only on contemporary reality that engulfs us, but on human condition as well. In "Felling a Tree" Kumar says,

> Humiliation is lethal
> when the victim has no weapons for defence,
> when you have to carry your own cross
> and you are your own pyre —
> fuel, flame and ashes.

Kumar's sympathy is always with the poor and innocence who are the victims of the society. The pavement-sleepers of Bombay, for whom the 'day is for sweating' and who sleep "under cover of night-sky/heads on jute-bags rolled into pillows," may look like 'corpses waiting to be dumped/into a mass grave' but, for the poet they 'are only fallen angels/ who will return home when the sun/ has run its course.'

Woolgathering gives vent to his memory and desire and makes an assertion of 'self' through dream and reality. Life, love, and death-three eternal themes of poetry are worked out artistically in this volume. The poet has come to terms with the mystery of life and declares in "On Listening to Mozart's Requiem" :

> I know when the wind waves its wand,
> it's time to give up.

The world of human beings is contrasted with the world of birds in the manner of Keats' poem "Ode to a Nightingale." "Talking to a Bird on my Window-sill" brings home the agony of life. People may change and smile but the agony abides, Kumar seems to say. Thus, he writes :

> You seem to chirp your way through life —
> never a streak of sorrow

in your beady eyes.
You don't know the problems I have to face —
darkness, rain, nightmares —
or that cyclone, last summer, that uprooted
a tree in my compound, demolishing
a nest that had sheltered my vagrant thoughts.

Kumar's poetry being image oriented, it falls into the category of 'Oblique Poetry' in contrast with 'Direct Poetry' which yields meaning at the surface level. Kumar's poetry makes sense at the deep level and therefore, irony becomes an important mode in his poetry.

Kumar's poems on Indian landscape are integrated with contemporary life in our society as in "Banaras : Winter Morning," "Dawnbreak over Khasi Hills," "Musings in a Park" and "Moongazing."

In 'Dawnbreak over Khasi Hills,' Kumar expresses the 'secret sorrows' of individuals as well as the tribes in terms of the landscape of the place. one finds a brilliant example of pathetic fallacy at work in the following lines :

Outside my window, a tall weeping
willow, its stable tresses drooping
from its shoulders,
is still immersed in some ancient
grief — its tears watering a fugitive
flower-bed beneath which I buried
my mother, three winters ago.
Out there, from the drowsy valley
rises a wall, bemoaning all those tribal
ancestors who walked away beyond the hills
centuries ago
lost in their secret sorrows.

Like the Tower Volume of W.B. Yeats, *Woolgathering* to mind, is Kumar' greatest poetic achievement. Here, there are memories of love and lost relationships, bitterness in married life, separation but all the dreams are not shattered and the hope is not completely lost. Instead, the poet has learnt the wisdom of life passing through the fire of suffering, pain and even betrayal. Again like Yeats, Kumar can be read as a poet of the old age who realises that 'ripeness is a cruel mentor' and knows 'it's only my mind sending out/skiffs down and bloodstream.' That Kumar has acquired the wisdom of Shakespeare ('ripeness is all') and Milton ('the mind in its own place and in itself can make a Heaven of Hell and a Hell of Heaven') — is for the discerning readers to see. Again in 'Walking by Riverside' he asserts that when 'the past and present eddy around each other/reinforcing nothingness,'. 'disaster comes too soon.'

Kumar's forthcoming book of verse, *Thus Spake the Buddha* (the MSS of the book was made available to me by the Poet) contains forty-one poems. Like the earlier books of verse, this volume also expresses the agony of the love for a woman. The distrust of a woman continues to haunt the mind of the poet. Like Shakespeare highlighting the friend in his sonnets, Kumar prefers to give a male friend and the woman the same weightage in a poem called, "A Letter to Sharad." As Kumar puts it :

> As though I could see two faces
> mirrored in my mind's pool,
> both floating in concentric circles
> yet each drawn to its own moon.
> One face to carry to bed
> when the blood leaps in the veins....
> And the other — that's your face —
> always there for a dialogue on time —
> past, present and future.

Having said this, the poet realizes that woman is not as trustworthy as a friend. Thus, he says,

> How far can you go with a woman
> to empathy? Misgiving and mistrust would
> yawn at every step, like pitfalls.

With the friend, it is different. The poet can go with the friend anywhere and any time. A true friend for him is 'a free gift from God' (Kumar says, so in an interview). Thus, there is a need to maintain a balance between a friend and a woman. He came to a conclusion :

> To close, let me improvise on Pythagoras
> Give me a lever long enough
> and I'll hold the universe evenly balanced
> between you and her :
>
> ('A Letter to Sharad')

Kumar also includes some topical poems in this book. Reference to Graham Staines' burning and oblique hint at Nissim Ezekiel's Alzheimer disease are cases in point. Graham Staines, an Ausralian missionary was burnt to death along with his two sons. This is an important incident in recent history, which deeply hurts the poet. He likens Graham Staines to Christ and his death to Christ's Crucifixion.

> Sundown. A van carrying him and his two sons
> is torched. A frantic struggle to escape
> but they're speared back into the interno.
> An anguished sky blazes a forked lightning
> to signal the end of innocence....
> when the media flashed his photograph,
> he looked like a prophet who'd walked
> over the Pacific waters, all the way
> from his land of Kangaroo, to seek
> crucifixion far away from home.
>
> ("Murder of a Missionary")

Ezekiel is virtually incapacitated because of the Alzheimer's disease and confined to a hospital. In 'Death of a Poet' Kumar writes about a poet who died of Alzheimer and whose wife dumped him in a nursing home prior to his death. Kumar writes :

> Long before his end, his wife had dumped
> him into the basement of a nursing home
> that he imagined to be the cellar chosen
> by the pharaoh of Hadad for his burial.

The hint at Ezekiel's case is unmistakable. If *Articulate Silences* begins with pain and sufferings in life, *Thus Spake the Buddha* marks the culmination of Kumar's realization of life and recognition of the 'self' that brings peace and happiness. He has now gained wisdom out of vast experiences of life. Hence, poems like "Lord Krishna to Arjuna," 'Renunciation' (already referred to in the introduction chapter of this book), "Vandana Weds Ramesh," "Meditation" and "Birds' Homecoming at Sunset" show Kumar's acceptance of the ways of life and an affirmation of his faith in divinity. These poems remind us of Eliot's *Four Quartets* in which he accepts life and wishes mankind well. Kumar now understands that in life "pain is born in mother's womb" and ends only with the ashes. And again, 'attachment generates only anguish.' To be successful life, we must 'act in the present, banshing all thoughts of the future,' says Kumar and the echo of Eliot's concept of time is unmistakable. Kumar comes very close to Eliot when he unravels the mystery of life in the concluding poems of *Thus Spake the Buddha*. Here are a few memorable lines :

> The way inside is the way out
> to understanding —
> that each paradox carries two faces :
> bud and insect, beginning and end.
>
> And beyond all this
> is pure void, neti —
> the essence of perennial tranquility.
> Shantih!
>
> ('Meditation')

> This is
> the moment to learn that giving is also
> taking — that to move forward
> one may have to retrace a step.
>
> I then see, in my mind's eye,
> two cranes up in the air,
> their wings flapping in unision in response

to some primal force that saves the cosmos
from falling apart
For the centre must hold, somehow.
('Vandana Weds Ramesh')

Kumar has come a longway from distrust between man and woman that bedevils life. Instead, he wishes man, and woman to come to terms with each other so that life will blossom. Men and women should live in harmony like the 'Sages lived in caves in harmony/with the wind rain, thunder/and the beasts' 'two millennia ago.' Kumar understands not only the pain and sufferings in life but joy of it in a philosophical sense. His poetry is a veritable apotheosis of passion and tragic affirmation of life. It is an achievement of a very high order that very few poets can aspire to.

WORKS CITED

Dulai, Surjit S. "Shiv K. Kumar's Writing." *Journal of South Asian Literature.* 25 : 2 (Summer, Fall 1990) : 9-48.

Kulshrestha, Chirantan. Ed. *Contemporary Indian English Verse : An Evaluation.* New Delhi : Arnold-Heinmann Publishers, 1980.

Kumar, Shiv K. *Woodpeckers*. London. Sidgwick and Jackson Ltd., 1979.

———. *Trapfalls in the Sky*. Madras : MacMillan India Ltd., 1986.

———. *Woolgathering*. Mumbai: Disha Books, 1998.

———. *Thus Spake the Buddha* (Forthcoming).

4

The Development of Technique

The art of writing poetry is linked with the themes that a poet chooses to write on. The language, the rhetoric, the imagery, the mode of expression, collocation of new words and use of symbols and myths go together to build the technique in poetry. For a post-colonial Indian English Poet, the creation of a new idiom and employment of new themes by way of resistance to the former coloniser are the two important ingredients of his poetry. Shiv K. Kumar is no exception. Kumar begins his poetic career with a desire to express his personal loss, pain and sorrow in the form of an art. But soon he broadened his poetic base by writing poems on East-West encounter, poems about contemporary life and society (topical poems), and above all specifically Indian poems that at once distinguish him from poets writing in English elsewhere in the world. Kumar excels as an ironist and parodist when he takes a dig at the corruption and injustice that one finds in our society. In this chapter, an attempt has been made to disscuss the imagery, irony, symbols and the idiom in Kumar's poetry.

In course of an interview given to Shyam Asnani, Kumar speaks candidly about the techniques employed in his poetry. 'Ironic perception or irony as a mode of perception is there in all my poems' says Kumar" (*Literature and Criticism* 1991-92 : 157).

Kumar makes use of irony as a mode of perceptional to expose the hollowness of rituals and religious practices. B.P. Parasher makes a pertinent observation on Kumar's use of irony in his religious poems :

"The poems in "Subterfuges" fall chiefly into three divisions : religious, amatory and autobiographical. The religious poems have a tone of inquiry about the glorified image of deities and of research into the practices which are seemingly vile but inherently good. With an uncanny insight Kumar seizes upon the reverse aspect of deities ('Kali' and 'The Sun Temple, Konarak'), sees sanctity in sex ('To A Prostitute') and sex encroaching upon devotion ('Wife at Prayer').

Kali is not a hymn but a discovery of polarities on three levels : divine, human and animal. Contrary to the maternal image the Kali is pre-eminently a deity of death feeding on her progeny, as the Black one, as the feminine form of the word Kala meaning Time, as one who begets and annihilates. She is creative and destructive, and the two contending aspects are the embodiment of one principle — the divine cosmic energy, of the human beings in whom the hunger for life has the implications of life and death and the animal world where the strongest feed on the weakest. This vulnerability of life is conveyed through the life-annihilating symbols — dog, serpent, hyena, the ravenous deity and the famished woman and the life-sustaining animals — child, lamb, mother and there are symbols which have partners in both the groups. If more than one meaning constitutes irony, then blood has its association with life and death : if it is a favourite drink of the Kali, it is also symbolic of energy and creation. It is by conjuring the ambivalent nature of the Kali that Kumar wonders at the process of creation and destruction and at the plight of man whose bloody neck is a temptation to the scavenger hyenas :

If the way to create
is the way to kill,
I have hoarded enough blood
in my throat
for all the hyenas to suck from.

The hunger for life and the seeming duality is tellingly reflected in the imagery of life and death, supported by the kindred ideas of construction and vandalism, poison and nectar" (JLA 2 : 4, 1982 : 42-43).

Common man in India believes in a holy communion with nature, and worships the Himalayas and the Ganges. Many of India's religious rites are performed on the banks of her holy rivers after ceremonial bathing. Aldous Huxley wrote a sarcastic essay on Varanasi in which he ridiculed Indians who took a dip in river Ganges. Like Huxley a rationalist Kumar could not share the blind beliefs of the masses and instead wrote some sarcastic poems on these rituals. His poems "Crematorium in Adikmet, Hyderabad," "At the Ghats of Banaras," "Pilgrimage," 'Kali,' and "An Encounter with Death" are cases in point. Beggars, priests and carnivorous animals together with vultures surrounded cremation places and Ghats of Banaras. Kumar refuses to be swayed away by mere rituals and instead sees the horror and reality within. He records these incidents with a subtle touch of irony and skilful art of sarcasm in the following manner :

> Incessant din of beggars
> and chants...
> Perched on the wall a vulture cogitates
> upon human avidity-flesh offered
> to the flames, bones and ashes
> to the Ganges. No leavings
> for the living ...
> The priest chants louder for a generous tip.
>
> (Crematorium in Adikmet, Hyderabad)

> Between its carrion teeth
> the Ganges can hold three live fishes-
> fins, bones, and eyes.
> A child's lissom body
> in a jute bag.
> the warm ashes of a young courtesan.
> and once I saw a man ferry across
> On a sleazy raft to drop

his pet dog and bless
the sharks that carried the prize away.

(At the Ghats of Banaras)

Kumar points out the futility of taking pilgrimages and warns :

We are out to span the sky's amplitude
this journey is merely to stimulate the blood.
The woman mumbled, 'Rest would be haven
— indeed.'
I was the only one to caution
that gods had trapped us
into belief.

(Pilgrimage)

Kumar describes the shocking things like animal sacrifices in a detached and dispassionate manner :

Beyond the priest's monotone
a lamb bleats for the knife-edge.
...but your nectar is the blood
that jets from fresh arteries.
If the way to create
is the way to kill,
I have hoarded enough blood
in my throat
for all the hyenas to suck from.

(Kali)

Kumar depicts the scene following his mother's death and the rituals that haunted him :

For thirteen days, say the Hindus, the departed
soul hovers round its earthly habitat, and
so for thirteen days I have communed with the
spirit — whenever a door-handle rattles, a
ripping wind howls, the dog whines or
blue-bells clang. I feel her presence within me.

(An Encounter with Death)

Kumar explains the idea behind his use of irony in his interview with Asnani (mentioned earlier in this chapter) in the following words :

"I relish debunking any form of intellectualism, pragmatism, religious posturing. Take the example of a priest : I want him to be simple, honest, austere and saintly. And here you have a priest who keeps on indulging in all sorts of worldly activities, including revelling in lust, wealth, debauchery. I belong to an orthodox religious family. My father was a devout theologian who had read the Vedas, the Quran and the Bible, and even he couldn't condition my responses. He later became a stauch Arya Samajist. I believe that religion's true experience is one where you are honest to yourself. You don't unnecessarily debunk or criticize others, but at the same time you can't go on accepting the hypocrisies of these professional priests, mullahs and monks. And religion as an institutionalised response — that's what I detest most. That's why, you see, when I encounter a mullah or a monk playing havoc with religion, I get intolerant, I cut him to size" (1992-93 : 157).

In "Cleansing Ganga" Kumar after describing the way we pollute Ganga, ironically suggests to cleanse the 'Ganga in us' before cleansing the river.

> At nativity all creatures are chaste, like breast-milk —
> ...
> it's only when they are carried down the river of time
> that iron sinks into their souls.
> The waters then get sullied by ritual and dogma-
> ashes and bones,
> wilted floral offerings to the dead.

Kumar himself explains the idea behind this poem in the following words :

'There my mode is subtly ironic. You see, there are Pandas sitting on the banks of the Ganga like crocodiles with their jaws wide open and chanting mantras. The idea is : why should religion be imagistic, an intimate conversation with God? And now many people understand the Sanskrit mantras. They are beautiful and embody beautiful thoughts. But once you don't understand their meaning and intent, the whole idea of religiousity is reduced to perfunctorily performing the rituals. So, in "Cleansing Ganga," the suggestion is to cleanse the Ganga in you of all orthodoxy, hypocrisy, and then initiate yourself into an intimate conversation with your deity in your prelapsarian innocence' (Ibidem : 157-158).

In 'Death of a Poet' the irony is implicit in the observation of the poet about a wife's reaction against her poet-husband's death.

> Good riddance, muttered his wife to herself
> as the pit swallowed his coffin
> patched up with planks and nails
> from some old furniture.

Kumar believes that irony can be successfully employed to make one see life in its clarity. He states :

"As I have said earlier, irony, wit, Puckish humour, impish smile or whatever you call it, is the only way to see life in all clarity because the only other alternative is sentimental, romanticized response to life. It is only through irony the artist can see through the chinks. You see through a priest, you see through a school master. There is a poem in 'The Broken Columns' about the school teacher who just drinks and carouses and mustaches. Irony, therefore, is a multifaceted weapon, a kind of poetic strategy which can be put to very effective use" (Ibidem : 151).

Imagery is an integral part of a poet's technique of writing poetry. For a post-colonial poet, the image of the native land is an important ingredient of his poetry. Kumar is not an exception. Telescoping of images drawn from Indian scenes forms an important part of Kumar's technique. Nothing attracts him more than the images of India in all walks of life. What makes Kumar an Indian and for that matter an Indian poet Indian, an Australian poet Australian, and an American poet

American, may be evident in the nature of the poet's response to the landscape (topographical as well as metaphysical) of his country as distinct from, or conjoined with, or merging into, an intellectual and religious tradition, wherever available. The Englishness of William Shakespeare, Wordsworth, John Keats and Tennyson lies in their intimacy with the English landscape. As Judith Wright has remarked very aptly :

"Before one's country can become an accepted background against which the poet's and novelist's imagination can move unhindered, it must first be observed, understood, described and, as it were, absorbed. The Writer must be at peace with his landscape before he can confidently turn to its human figures" (Das 1993 : 53).

In this context the theme of landscape and national identity makes a rewarding study when applied to Shiv K. Kumar. In him one detects a certainty of touch that seems to reflect a confidence in the direction and purpose of his writing, as well as an integrity of images of India, style and subject matter. Kumar's imaginative world derives its power to involve the reader from its rich mimetic content while its enduring quality comes from the verbal imagery drawn from many sources. Thus he grapples with ideas and abstractions, images of men and women on several plains, the complex of emotions centering round human activities such as love, sex, companionship and problems relating to his own art. The poet's primary commitment is to the image and symbol through which he apprehends reality.

"Images of 'India' are handled with a consummate skill and keenness of intellect in Kumar's specifically Indian poems like, 'Indian women' , 'An Indian Mango Vendor,' 'Transcendental Meditation,' 'A Hindu to his Cow,' 'Rickshaw-wallah,' 'My Correspondent,' 'Karma' and 'Aftermath.' 'Kumar's treatment of the theme of love (*i.e.*, man and woman relationship) in terms of the elements of the Indian landscape has the weight of a poetic reconciliation of the spirit and the country. He incorporates the heat and dust, the sun and flood, the crowd, the sense of poverty and deprivation into the texture of his moods" (Ibidem : 57).

Like Ramanujan, Kumar chooses appropriate titles for his poems which reveal Indian sensibility. In 'Indian Women,' Kumar likens the Indian Women to empty pitchers on villages wells, for they wait anxiously 'for their men's return' with patience as the latter wait to be filled in. In "An Indian Mango Vendor," Kumar re-creates a bazar scene in which women sells mangoes while some customers eye on her. The evocative scene is described with insight.

She squats
on the dust-broomed pavement
behind a pyramid of mangoes
washed with her youth's milk
tinctured with the musk-rose in her hair.
Through the slits
of her patched blouse
one bare shoulder
two white moons
pull all horses
off the track.
This old man's leery eyes —

In 'At the Ghats of Banaras' the poet describes a scene tinged with irony to say how rituals are performed at the Ghats of Banaras

A priest's chant
tender but peremptory
churns the viscid waters
into submission

Similarly Kumar lashes out the judicial system that is prevalent in this country for its failure to mete out justice to the petitioners in time. The caustic observations marked by irony bring home the inherent lacuna in our judicial system. Kumar writes ;

Born out of the moon's eye —
tender, omniscent, lithe-limbed —
justice was ambushed mid-air,
pulled down to these chambers

then nourished on casuistry and deferment.
Now she speaks a dialect nobody can understand.

The cases drag on for years and waiting seems to be endless. Kumar sarcastically brings out the Kaurava-Pandava dispute as an analogy to show how people suffer for centuries to get justice. Thus, he writes :

There's the Kaurava-Pandava land-wrangle
still being argued in some haunted chamber —
....
It's the long wait that kills
the lover, the cancer-patient
and the petitioner.

(Tis Hazari Courts, Delhi)

The poem is evocative of the Court scene in our country and reminds us of a drawback that is inherent in our judicial system.

As a humanistic poet, Kumar's sympathies lie with the suffering humanity. He brings a contrast between the innocence and suffering of the poor on the one hand and arrogance and pride of the rich on the other in a poem called, "Pavement-sleepers of Bombay." The imagery employed in the poem is adequate to the situation and infact the image becomes the idea. Poverty is reflected in the body. Kumar describes :

Lying cheek by jowl, under cover of night-sky,
heads on jute-bags rolled into pillows,
legs dangling on the curb,
they look like corpses waiting to be dumped
into a mass grave

The pavement-sleepers may be poor but they have peace of mind which is beyond the reach of a rich woman 'in her maroon Mercedes' and the priests. Hence, Kumar brings out the sharp contrast in clear cut terms :

That woman, in her maroon Mercedes,
drunk on speed, doesn't know
that the road she has taken leads nowhere
that peace resides on these pavements

that while an empty belly's prayer
is echoed by the stars, the priest's vespers
never rise beyond the cathedral's dome
because these sleepers are only fallen angels
(Pavement-sleepers of Bombay)

Kumar brings out a contrast between the two worlds of birds and human beings. The echo of Keats' "Ode to a Nightingale" is distinct in Kumar's "Talking to a Bird on my window-sill." Kumar writes :

You seem to chirp your way through life —
never a streak of sorrow
in your beady eyes.
You don't know the problems I have to face —
darkness, rain, nightmares —
or that cyclone, last summer,....

And unlike human beings the birds are not haunted by man-made laws and harassed by the authorities. The rhetorical questions bring out the contrast between the poetic-persona and the bird in the following lines :

If you were also dislodged
from your native soil,
how long would it take you to move
to a new abode? ...
... Are you also
haunted by the dread of a night-raid
demanding a declaration of all your assets?

The harassment of common and decent people at the hands of people who are supposed to uphold law hurts Kumar and he depicts such a scene in "Moongazing."

But now the masked
intruders zoom in, like ravens, as if to find
some evidence of stolen property
from their planet where suspicion
worms into everyone's brain
like a malignant tumour.

On seeing only vast expanses of loneliness
and dust, craters spilling over
with ennui
they withdrew
into their guilt. But not
without carrying away a baby-rock
as if it were the Kohinoor
from Golconda, to justify their invasion
of a neighbour's territory.

The similies employed in the above passage are appropriate to the context and the implicit irony inherent in the comparisons is poignant. The images drawn from human diseases and history of the nation are adequate to convey contemporary reality in artistic terms.

Kumar excels in creating new images. In the title poem of his forthcoming volume 'Thus Spake the Buddha,' Kumar creates startling images to drive home the disastrous consequences of human desire.

Desire lights its own pyre
and even water fuels it.
I see in the time's womb
round a millennium's bend
a potentate who lets a cobra
into the oval chamber of his white
palace, only to be stung all over —
and noosed by history
with his own scarf.

("Thus Spake the Buddha")

Kumar employs innovative images in his later poetry. The feeling of a child in the womb before birth and after the delivery is conveyed to us in subtle images.

Anchored to the navel, I lie coiled
head between the thighs —
sustained, like someone marooned

on a remote island,
by food dropped from the air.

And after birth the child thought that it would be 'exposed to public scrutiny.' Thus, it is,

time to learn a new language
spruced by syntax, parentheses and periods —
though devious like a whore's smile,
slick like a seal's skin.

('Inside the Womb')

Kumar employs images with insight to explain the idea inherent in the theme of the poem, as in "Putting an Old Sick Dog to Sleep." Sleep is used as metaphor for death. Kumar describes the last days of the dog with wit that arrests the readers' imagination.

...he lay gasping
For three days he hadn't touched his bowl
of milk, as if he'd renounced his life —
sustaining oxygen to cross the river
of time to a land where man, bird and trees
spoke the same language....
I understood it was now time to summon
the man with lethal syringe that freezes
all movement....
...I visualized
death creeping surreptitiously through
his intestines, heart and face. And as his eyelids
dropped. I heard a voice in the year
Would you take me again, Master
if I'm reborn as a puppy?

I felt as though the dams behend the sockets of my eyes burst and the floods submerged the entire planet.

The imagery is drawn from various sources to reinforce the idea. The humanism in the poet transcends the individual in him and acquires a kind of universality in which any man anywhere in the world can empathize. The visual imagery of eyes bursting with tears and flooding the planet is poignant and apt in the context. Moreover, the philosophical idea of man, bird and tree becoming one (*i.e.*, speaking 'the same language') after death is reinforced in the protagonist's pining for the loss at the death of the sick dog.

In 'Depression' Kumar employs images that convey in no uncertain terms the consequences of depression in life. In the beginning he likens depression to 'tidal wave' that comes and goes and 'hits a lone island' and then to 'a kite cut loose from its string/swings upside, down/in the autumn wind' and finally it creates a 'void that resembles Yama/in The Book of the Dead.' This is an oblique poem in which Kumar implicitly suggests that depression if not checked in time may lead to death.

Depression also springs from the failure in love. Kumar's imagistic skill is heightened by the desire to consummate love and the failure to achieve it. He is haunted by the human body which he seeks in fragments and 'out of joint' rather than an organic whole. Thus, in 'Gynous Truth,' 'the nipples bend the vanquished muscles' and the thighs of the prostitutes in 'To a Prostitute' are 'forespent thighs' and 'The Sun Temple, Konarak,' reveals the 'riotous sea of navesls, breasts/and lips.' This prompted G.S. Amur to say that "the images of dismemberment transferred to the human body are a recurrent feature of his imagery" (Naik 1979 : 134). Kumar is so much preoccupied with the human body that even while chanting from the Gita, at his father's behest, he could smell the 'Puff of deodar rustles/through a girl's skirt' and imagines sex-all between two tender legs that 'gyrate the air into fuzzy yearnings.' A girl's body is likened to the Bay of Bengal in the III Section of "Broken Columns" where the Poet says :

> I transfix her behind a pillar
> of deodar and my lips
> release the tongue to plumb
> the Bay of Bengal.

Kumar does not glorify woman in his poetry. The purpose of describing human anatomy is to show 'the skull beneath the skin.' Kumar deromanticizes the conventional and stock response to woman as an object of beauty. I concur with B.P. Parashar's observation on this point :

"Woman — a paragon of beauty and virtue, a constant concern of the amorous poetry is demythicised in Shiv K. Kumar. She is shorn of her romantic trappings, relegated to the commonplace pedestal and associated with the disease which hampers the bloom of love. The disease manifests itself in ogling, adultery, cuckoldry, infidelity, disharmony in conjugal relations, permissive sex, hired sex and rape. She is not a fervent lady-love courting perils for love but a calculating lady, more worried about her heat than about the ecstacy of love, a patient with ailing body who is incapacitated for the culmination of the sexual act, a jejune spinster who loses her teeth before she knows love, a desperate lady who conceives dreams for a child without capacity for conception, a cabaret dancer who, unmindful of leprous clients, kisses them, not out of love, but out of sheer obligation" (JLA 1982 : 2 : 4, 45).

Kumar's wit and humour enliven his poetry. There are moments of realisation in his poetry such as in "Vandana Weds Ramesh."

As a flame
rises from a camphor in a broken coconut that
looks like the palm of some deity
the ritual begins to unfold its mystique.
...
A hush descends upon everyone
as I'm asked to make an offering of the bride
to the brown god beside her. This is
the moment to learn that giving is also
taking — that to move forward
one may have to retrace a step.

The paradox employed in the last two lines quoted above amply illustrates Kumar's insight into life and his wit to portray things that are happening around us. He creates new images in artistic terms. Thus, he writes :

Eternally serene —
because his mind is a tortoise
that has withdrawn all its outposts
under its steel umbrella.

('Meditation')

Kumar creates innovative images by likening rain to someone's rinsing and saint's tears. Rain is taken as a symbol of regret-something unusual in our situation, as shown in the following lines :

Someone is rinsing the sky's azure bedspread
or is it some saint in tears
who fell for a woman with the eyes of a gazelle.
Twenty years of meditation
Squandered away.

("Watching the Rain from My Balcony")

In 'Midnight Musings' thighs are likened to eucalyptus and despair knows no age. As Kumar puts it.

The moment of despair
has no age
no discretion

At fifty-two I see eucalyptus
thighs waiting to be hustled
by mere sunset.

In "Cabaret Dancer' Kumar uses subtle images to suggest the arousal of sexual desire seeing a cabaret dancer performing on the stage. Kumar writes :

A frenzied moan curls up
from Hades and all
the animals are unleashed.
A scramble for a closer
scrutiny of the deity.

Kumar is adept at creating learned imagery-often farfetched like the English Metaphysical poets. He puts his vast experience and learning into the making of original images in his poetry. Wit and ingenuity combine in his poetry to produce startling images as in poems like 'To a Young Beautiful Woman Aspiring to be a Poet' and 'Khajuraho.'

> Do you know that your upper lip's cresent
> may tempt even a muezzin to break his fast
> before the moonrise
> and incite the placid Mediterranean to insurgency?...
>
> In any case, writing a poem is like breaking
> a genie into doing a tantric ritual.
> Even the Sphinx was struck dumb, not knowing
> how to solve the riddle
> of clipping the wings
> of a wanton simile
>
> ('To a Young Beautiful Woman Aspiring to be a Poet')

The above quoted lines suggest the charm of a girl that can break the fast of a muezzin and the inscrutability of the art of writing poetry. The images are not only new but startling as well. Kumar has an inwardness with language and image making power and therefore, one finds new coinage of words and innovative images in his poetry.

The beauty of Khajuraho is described in an artistic way in the following lines :

> Here the sculptor's hands
> have forged wanton patterns
> witnessed by bird, goat and priest
> as in every cosmic gyre
> the entire creation participates.

This reminds us of Tennyson's lines in "In Memoriam" when the poet says, 'there is only one God ... /around which the whole creation moves.'

The image of the sea as a woman — a feminine reproductive principle, is portrayed artistically to show how all creation began with her. The personification of the sea as a woman reminds us of the origin of life and as Kumar rightly states :

It all began with the sea
from whose womb sprang up
rock, fish and oil.

She's always willing to take anyone,
anytime. If during day, she lets, the Sun
spray his liquid gold on her body
at night, the moon may dive into her
for her nocturnal bath — a virgin
in her nude splendour, with only a passing
cloud to veil her from prying eyes.

("Cottage on the Beach")

Kumar being a humanistic poet seeks truth in life but not beyond it. At the same time he is not blind to the human intricacy that spoils life and perpetuates bitterness. He likes the mountains for they celebrate life and takes 'love' as a source of sustenance in life in the sameway as Matthew Arnold did in "Dover Beach." Thus, in a poem titled, 'The Himalayas' Kumar depicts his idea of truth and love in the following way :

It's not on top of the Everest
that truth resides
but below its roots ....

Love, not the sun, is real
sustenance to seed, fruit, flower
and the soul.

Each mountain may look like
some Pharaoh's tomb
but it celebrates life
not doom.

No wonder these mountains have chosen
to stay away from the plains
where rhetoric masquerades as logos
and every road-sign leads one into the
blind alley of polemic and denial.

("The Himalayas")

Love and the consummation of love are visually reproduced on the temple walls of Konarak and Khajuraho. Kumar writes :

Indeed, there would be time
to consummate the ritual, later at night,
in a deluxe room at the Hill View
that has witnessed scenes
from Konarak and Khajuraho.

('Honeymooners' Lane, Kodaikanal')

The sexual imagery is carried further, when love for the poet has become, 'a pneumatic bout of love' as in 'Aftermath' and dreams have become 'abortive dreams' as is 'Kovalam Beach.' To him the bodies are 'diabetic bodies' and there is no orgasm in sex-act (which is the peak of it) but a 'semblance of orgasm.' Lusty-eyes ogling at the nude female model are termed 'The fox's eye' and the female anatomy is likened to the vast horizon. Thus, the poet says :

The horizon's waist line
wrinkles round a dark shore
whence a tired eye peers
at vacancies

(Nude Model in Art Class)

In Kumar's poetry one encounters erotic images, which bears a parallel to the sexual images of Kamala Das. For instance, images like, 'Vaginal Creeks,' 'semen of primeval gods,' 'blue veined breasts,' 'silken thighs' (a borrowing from T.S. Eliot's 'Silken Girls' in 'Journey of the Magi') and "nipples smeared with gold dust-powder/swing hysterically/round swaying waist lines," are very daring and un-conventional.

The figures of speech that are associated with these images heightens the meaning and musicality of the poem, "Buddha at a Night Club." For instance, the last image just quoted above, is helped by figures of speech like transferred epithet (breasts swing histerically) and alliteration (swing/swaying) to evoke the sensual appeal of the dancer at a night club.

Kumar's technique of writing poetry is in direct current of Post-colonial Indian English Poetry beginning with Nissim Ezekiel.

The choice of words, the employment of imagery, the fondness for metaphor — all go together to build a technique of his own in Kumar's poetry. Frequent use of similes and metaphors, wit and indigenous imagery, and aboveall, Kumar's concentration on the subject and the logic behind his argument give his poetry an identity (should we say, 'a local habitation and a name?') that is both lovable and enduring. Kumar, like Eliot also makes use of foregrounding in his poetry like 'forespent thighs' in "To a Prostitute." His vast learning and scholarship of English literature — particularly that of Shakespeare and Eliot go a longway to build a poetic style of his own. The echoes of Shakespeare and Eliot are heard frequently. Take for example, his poem 'Birth of my Son,' where he writes :

> In the beginning was the cry
> not the word. But didn't it sound
> like a loud protest against what was to follow?

This reminds us of Shakespeare's words, "When we are born we cry because we have come to a great stage of fools." Paradoxical statements and anti-thesis abound in Kumar's Poetry as in Eliot's 'Four Quartets.' References to 'Bhagabat Gita' in a poem called "Lord Krishna to Arjuna" is reminiscent of Eliot's 'Four Quartets.' Kumar also echoes some of Nissim Ezekiel's ideas and employs his strategies in quite a few of his poems. Shakespeare's 'the lunatic — the lover and the poet,' Ezekiel's "the poet — the lover and the bird watcher" seem to have influenced Kumar to create a syndrome like, 'the lover, the cancer — patient and the petitioner' in "Tis Hazari Courts, Delhi." This is not to suggest that Kumar is an inferior poet. Chaucer, Shakespeare, Eliot — all have borrowed ideas and imagery from several sources. It is not important what a poet borrows but what he does with his borrowings. Chaucer, Shakespeare, Eliot all have borrowed skeletons from several sources but they have injected flesh and blood into their borrowings. As a result, their poetry became lively, vigorous and enjoyable, so is the case with Shiv K. Kumar. Kumar being a Professor of English brings all his knowledge of English literature and literatures in English (including American Literature) into the realms of his poetry. Thus, his poetry becomes vibrant and enjoyable. Is not it, Eliot who said, "Immature poets immitate, mature poets steal?" Kumar's poetry with its innovative imagery and learned vocabularly may appear difficult at the surface level but as one dives deep into the deep structure, the hard shell of the coconut gets ruptured, the sweet kernel emerges and satisfies the quench of the reader.

The quest of Kumar's poetry is a quest for peace. Passing through the pangs of suffering the mind needs peace. That is what he pines for in the following lines :

> So why not let the mind slide deep
> into some dark tunnel, to its farthest end
> where all questioning sounds futile.
> Peace. Withdrawal from all fronts.
>
> (Lazing on the Lawn, Winter Morning)

The realisation comes in 'Meditation' and Kumar finally comes to terms with life. Like Eliot, Kumar realises in the end that :

> The way inside is the way out
> to understanding —
> that each paradox carries two faces :
> bud and insect, beginning and end.
> And beyond all this
> is pure void, neti
> the essence of perennial tranquillity
> Shantih!

WORKS CITED

Amur, G.S. "Poetry as Subterfuge : An Introduction to Shiv K. Kumar's Poetry." Aspects of Indian Writing in English. Ed. M.K. Naik. Madras : MacMillan, 1979.

Asnani, Shyam. "Interview with Shiv K. 'Kumar." Literature and Criticism I : 1-2, 1991-92.

Das, Bijay Kumar. Quoted. *Critical Essays on Poetry*. New Delhi : Kalyani Publishers, 1993.

Parashar, B.P. "Aesthetics of Irony in Shiv K. Kumar," Journal of Literature and Aesthetics. 2 : 4, 1982.

5

Postcoloniality and Shiv K. Kumar's Poetry

In this chapter I propose to place Shiv K. Kumar on the map of postcolonial poetry in the global context in the light of his achievements as a post-colonial Indian English Poet. Therefore, it is imperative on my part to define some protean terms like 'Postcolonialism,' 'Imperialism,' 'Orientalism,' 'Colonialism' and 'Postcoloniality' before evaluating Kumar as a Post-colonial poet.

Imperialism refers to the authority both political and military assumed by a state or a country over another territory. This term is associated with the expansion of European nations (particularly Great Britain) in the nineteenth century. In otherwords, imperialism means the dominance of one state over another territory for political subjugation and economic exploitation. Imperialism is both political and cultural as the conquering state imposes its culture on the conquered territory. On the other hand, colonialism means the consolidation of imperial power and "is manifested in the settlement of territory, the exploitation or development of resources, and the attempt to govern the indigenous inhabitants of occupied lands" (Boehmer 1995 : 2).

Orientalism is meant by what the West thinks about the East. It established the cultural superiority of the West over the East and paved the way for imperialism. "The essence of Orientalism is the ineradicable distinction between Western superiority and Oriental inferiority," says Edward Said (1991 : 16). If orientalism anticipated imperialism, the latter looked forward to colonialism which involves consolidation of imperial power and settlement of territory, exploitation of resources of indigenous people and ruling over them. Postcolonialism helps the native inhabitants to take their own place by achieving independence and overcoming political and cultural imperialism.

Colonial literature means the literature written by the native people including the writings by creoles and indigenous writers during colonial times. It is concerned with colonial perceptions and experience. On the other hand, colonialist literature is based on the theory of the superiority of European culture (*i.e.*, imperial culture) and the rightness of the empire. Post-colonial literature, (as the-nomenclature suggests), means the literature written after the withdrawal of the imperial power from the territory of the native people. Elleke Boehmer gives an interesting account of this literature in the following lines :

"Rather than simply being the writing which 'came after' empire, postcolonial literature is that which critically scrutinizes the colonial relationship. It is writing that sets out in one way or another to resist colonialist perspectives. As well as a change in power, decolonization demanded symbolic overhaul, a reshaping of dominant meanings. Post-colonial literature formed part of that process of overhaul. To give expression to colonized experience, post-colonial writers sought to undercut thematically and formally the discourses which supported colonization — the myths of power, the race classifications, the imagery of subordination. Post-colonial literature, therefore, is deeply marked by experiences of cultural exclusion and division under empire. Especially in its early stages it can also be a nationalist writing. Building on this, postcoloniality is defined as that condition in which colonized peoples seek to take their place, forcibly or otherwise, as historical subjects. Following more recent usage, the postcolonial must be distinguished from the more conventional hyphenated term post-colonial" (1995 : 3).

Like the term 'post-modernity,' 'post-coloniality' emphasizes a contemporary state and is currently in fashion with the literary critics. It atonce operates at two levels — first, as a historical marker of the period following decolonization and second, as an embodiment of intellectual approaches which have been influenced by post-structuralism and post-deconstruction. And what is more, in the late 1980s and early 1990s the term postcolonial has been used to replace the earlier terms like 'Third World' or 'Commonwealth Literature' The term Commonwealth Literature fell into rough weather in the hands of writers from the erstwhile British colonies, when it was drawn upon them that the writers of the colonizer (*i.e.,* England) do not form a part of this body of Literature. Hence, a new term post-colonial literature is coined to suggest de-centering of colonial literature. Two books, *The Empire Writes Back* (1987) by Ashcroft, Griffiths and Tiffin and *The Encyclopedia of Post-colonial Literatures in English* (1994) edited by Benson and Connolly proved to be the last nail in the coffin of Commonwealth Literature and popularized the term post-colonial literature.

Rajnath gives an account of the origins of postcolonial theory in the following words :

"The origins of postcolonial theory are rather complex. Did it emerge out of the ruins of poststructuralism? Was it a version of Marxism? Was it a reaction against formalism? Said's relationship with other critics and critical trends is far from simple. He has acknowledged the influence of Foucault who is both a structuralist and post-structuralist. For his political emphasis he can be clubbed with Marx. He has not dismissed formalism but finds it inadequate, just as he finds poststructuralism and Marxism inadequate. Nevertheless, the best way to view Said's postcolonial theory is to see it as a reaction against formalism, particularly Anglo-American New Criticism which ignored worldliness of a text. Whereas formalism focused on the pristine text with no affiliation to the author or the reader, let alone the world, Said's intervention brings in the world with a vengeance. The publication of 'Literature and Society' in 1980 edited by Said marked a significant mutation an Anglo-American criticism. In his 'Introduction' to the volume Said expressed acquiescence in the critical position taken by the contributors to the volume, which goes contrary to the New Critical stand. Said's own magnum opus 'Culture and Imperialism' published in 1993, brings out with considerable emphasis the political subtext of the mainstream Western writing" (JLC 9 : 1, 2000 : 73).

Postcolonial Indian English poetry makes its presence felt in the English speaking world by breaking a new ground both in themes and techniques. It can also be taken as a form of resistance to the former coloniser. Postcoloniality as Leela Gandhi rightly suggests is another name for globalisation. In other words, East-West encounter becomes a favourite theme for postcolonial Indian English poets. Shiv K. Kumar himself underlines this aspect of postcolonial Indian English poetry in the following words :

"Another recurring theme in most contemporary Indian Poetry in English is East-West cultural encounter. This perhaps relates to the fact that several of our poets have had their education abroad — at Oxford, Cambridge, Leeds or some American University. So they often tend to write like expatriates or exiles while living in the West and look back nostalgically on their Western experience when they return home" (Kumar 1992 : 5).

Postcolonial Writers (Poets included) overcome cultural imperialism by assimilating the foreign culture into their native culture. Our poets have enriched their experience and broadened their cultural outlook because of their interaction with the West. Ihab Hassan, a postcolonial critic asserts this point in the following words :

"Concerning cultural imperialism, I can speak more confidently : I am an example of it, and do not suppose that my life in Egypt would have been infinitely richer there than it is now in America. More I advocate cultural 'impurity,' that is the complex process of cultural indebtedness, of adaptation, cooptation, appropriation, assimilation — let us simply say translation — as well as refusal" (JLC 9 : 1, 2000 : 30). Hassan further quotes Eliot to say that cultural isolation comes from the lack of reciprocity in the following lines :

"I (Eliot) have suggested that national culture which isolates itself voluntarily or the national culture which is cut off from others by circumstances which it cannot control, suffers from this isolation. Also, that the country which receives culture from abroad without having anything to give in return and the country which aims to impose its culture on another without accepting anything in return, will both suffer from this lack of reciprocity" (Ibidem).

Edward Said reinforces the idea when he argues that, "Cultures are hybrid and heterogenous and...that cultures and civilizations are so interrelated and interdependent as to beggar any unitary or simply delineated description of their individuality" (Orientalism 1978 : 348-49). The interdependence of cultures and civilizations brings the West closer to the East and this fact cannot be wished away.

In "A Letter from Newyork" Kumar brings out the dichotomy between the East and the West and finally longs for returning home. As he puts it :

> Here I live in a garbage can
> and the pile grows bigger each week
> with the broken homes
> splintered all around.

Then comes the contrast between the two :

> They wouldn't believe it here
> that the Ganges' water can work
> miracles like Lourdes,'
> in spite of the cartloads of dead men's ashes.
> And bones and the pundits' shit —
> daily offerings to the Mother River!

The desire to glorify the West is no more. On the other hand, the protagonist notes that 'the white of the negro maid's eyebells is the only clean thing here' and asserts, 'but my soul is still my own.' And again, the protagonist knows that he can never be an American and longs to return home. And Kumar puts it succintly :

> But the brown of my skin defies
> all bleachers.
> How long will the eclipse last?

This reminds us of R. Parthasarathy's *Rough Passage* where the protagonist returns home putting an end to 'exile' in London. Like Parthasarathy, Kumar sees the ugliness, and deprivation in foreign society and describes it. In the West, one lives in an 'inverted manhole' or 'a garbage can' with 'broken homes/ splintered all around.' The colonial mind eulogizing the West for everything is no more. The post-colonial Indian English poets including Shiv K. Kumar don't hesitate to expose the myth of the superiority of the West over the East in an unambiguous way. Thus, Kumar is no more enamoured of London where he finds :

> There's no vent-hole in this bastille
> to subdue the fetor of putrescent
> flesh and bone, the sweat of
> humans fleeing from their shadows.
>
> (A Reminiscence)

The loss of the glory of the colonial power and its decrepitude makes the poet see into the life of things and therefore, Kumar says,

> Round the corner
> down a spurious lane
> the British Council's catacombs —
> remnants of a lost empire —
> shiver in this mild winter.
>
> ('Trafalgar Square')

Our political freedom brought along with it our cultural freedom from the coloniser. Kumar underlines this aspect in no uncertain terms :

"I may, therefore, say that we won not only our political independence in 1947, but also our cultural freedom as evidenced by a distinct change of attitude in our creative writers-poets, novelists and dramatists. This manifests a new consciousness of their roots as also of their own cultural heritage. It is this new vision that distinguishes their work from that of their predecessors. The new poets want poetry to be authentic, intensely personal, and written in a language shorn of cliches and verbosity. A poem, for them, must be a skilfully structured artefact of both image and emotion, thought and feeling" (1992 : 1-2).

Like other postcolonial poets, Kumar writes about the contemporary reality around us. His conception of morality is unconventional. He sees through the hypocrisy inherent in our socio-religious customs and seeks to expose it in his poetry.

In course of an interview given to Indian Literary Review Kumar states candidly his conception of God. He says :

"In the U.S.A., I began to read the Bible and everything had a double meaning. I said, "This is funny." In "Genesis," the moment you come to know good and evil you're banished. What kind of God is He that He doesn't want you to understand reality and know the truth, denies you the privilege to eat the fruit of the tree of knowledge. He wants to keep humans ignorant. What was the mysterious intention in the Maker's mind? There is a kind a conspiracy against human beings. So, I created my own Adam and Eve. In the garden of Eden, I imagine Adam and Eve making love to each other the first time. Then Eve speaks out, telling Adam : We were always there together, but never knew this! So it's my own attempt to transmute, to alchemise that experience. Nothing more" (JSAL : 237).

In "A Woman Labourer Breast-feeding her child, during lunch-break," Kumar speaks of the pure maternal love for a child. A woman labourer does her work and looks after her child at the same time. Love and duty enjoin her and she becomes a symbol of simplicity and innocence. Thus Kumar writes :

> Under her head-veil, now dropped
> to cover two moons, wee hands
> and feet flutter like a culver.

Time that never ceases to nibble
at stone, wood or glass
now pricks up its ears to listen
to a heart-throb.

In another poem, "Mother Teresa Feeds her Lepers at her Home for the Destitute, Calcutta" Kumar brings a contrast between Mother Teresa's pure love for the patients and destitutes in her Home for the Destitute and the way we worship 'a goddess in stone' in a temple. He believes that Mother Teresa is a real goddess — she is love personified.

This is how Kumar puts it :

When in love
go mute like pebbles under crystal
water, wear white silk, or take
the veil. Your eyes will then glow like fire-
flies, your footsteps fall like dew-
drops on banana leaves on a summer morn.
You may then leap through a ring of fire, kiss
a cobra's hood, work miracles with sand.
for you are then the Virgin's bridesmaid —
only half mortal like the lotus.

Across the street, a temple
peals out its chants, frightening away
the birds. Inside, a goddess in stone-
face ebony, eyes the colour of blood-
raises her right hand, like a cactus
blade, to consummate
an ancient ritual.

If post-colonial literature (poetry included) is the result of the interaction between imperial design and national culture on the one hand and 'imperial language and local experience' on the other, Shiv K. Kumar has little to fear. The ancient art is brought alive in Kumar's poetry when he successfully depicts the spirit of *Kamasutra* in verse :

Rhythm and fire —
this riotous sea of navals, breasts
and lips will never break
into prevarication
for the perfect logos
is the act
of affirmation.

('The Sun Temple, Konark')

The significance of a cow to the Hindus is underlined in the poem, 'A Hindoo To His Cow.' The holiness of the cow is linked with the holiness of the river Ganges in the following words :

Let them go beefing
around the coasts
from insects to mammals
from Hudson to Volga —
your mystique
only the Ganges will comprehend.

The Hindu idea of rebirth and regeneration is clearly shown in the poem "And Death Shall Speak With Many Voices." Death leads to a new life and the ashes of the deadbody which are carried away by winds attract the attention of the poet. The hope of a new life is uppermost in the minds of the people who subscribe to the Hindu view of life. Thus, Kumar writes :

The flamingoes may now
pick the unresonant bones
The ashes are waiting
for the stray winds.

("And Death Shall Speak with Many Voices")

The faith of the people (*i.e.*, the Hindus) in God and the choice of holy places for communion with God are shown in a subtle way in a poem called "Banaras : Winter Morning." Here, Kumar has come a longway from debunking the priests for chanting louder for a generous trip as in "Creamatorium at Adikmet, Hyderabad" or "At the Ghats of Banaras," and realised the significance of holy moments in one's life. Thus, he writes :

> Before dawn surrenders its last outpost
> to sun's copper ....
>
> This hour is sacrosanct —
> even the crow feigns cooing
> lest his cawing provoke blasphemy
> in the hallowed air ....
>
> If I were to die
> this is the moment
> and this the place.
>
> (Banaras : Winter Morning)

Cultural identities are points of identification and a form of resistance to be found within the discourses of history and culture. Kumar dives deep into history to recall Buddha's Renunciation and tell the readers about the ageold Indian wisdom of the cause of suffering and pain in life. The moment of Buddha's exit from his house and leaving the world for good is described with a romantic touch which is impulsive in thought but resolute in action. Thus, writes Kumar :

> Through a latticed window, the spring
> breeze glides into the bed-chamber,
> redolent of the jasmines in the garden below.
>
> On a thistledown bed, she's gone deep
> into a dream — an infant's head on her
> left breast, her right hand stretched in vain
> into the other hemisphere, as he has slipped
> off quietly to the door.
>
> A brief pause, as he darts a glance
> at his wife and son —
> But a voice summons him : "The moment
> in your horoscope is inexorable."
>
> ('Renunciation')

When Buddha got his enlightenment, he came back to his place to preach his religion. He has become an enlightened soul and understood the cause of pain and suffering in life. Thus, describes Kumar :

He puts out his bowl : "An offering
of your son, please. For who else would
understand what the bodhi tree
whispered into my ears?"

She smiles, knowing that he has travelled
through the marine world, nine fathoms
deep — and the space above the stars.
Pain, he has now learnt, is born
in the mother's womb, and ends only
when the ashes are silenced
by a sprinkling of milk.

This happened, more than two millennia ago
when sages lived in caves, in harmony
with the wind, rain, thunder —
and the beasts.

('Renunciation')

Kumar, who began his poetic career with articulating pain and sufferings in his personal life, has now, finally understood that pain is universal and inescapable. He realises that suffering is an integral part of human life and will remain so till the end of human civilization. Expressing one's self through national myths is one of the important ways in which a poet establishes his identity and a post-colonial poet expresses his resistance to the imperialistic culture. Kumar refers to Arjun's questions and Lord Krishna's answer just before the Mahabharat War to show the validity of ancient Indian wisdom. Thus, writes Kumar :

O Lord,
Can an act be divorced from the thought
of recompense?

That's man's ultimate frailty, O Warrior,
to know what lies beyond the horizon,
to know the end even before the beginning,
to know if the seed would sprout
into a leaf, and the leaf into a bud —
if a traveller would reach his destination

before sunset. No, you'd never know
what lies ahead because I hold this card
close to my chest. Or, or put it differently,
it lies in a sealed capsule under the ocean's
bed, inaccessible to man.

('Lord Krishna to Arjuna')

When Arjun was convinced he answered the questions with confidence. Thus, writes Kumar :

No more questioning, O Lord.
I can now read your message between the folds
of a rose, unravel the mystery of the blemish
on the moon's face, walk through a dense
forest at night, without the pole star's taper.

Then pick up your bow and arrow, O Warrior,
and fight to set the crooked straight.
Your destiny was etched on your palm
at birth. Just as it was preordained
that I accompany you, like the musk
in a deer's navel — a whisper in the air
that leads a lone traveller through a wilderness.
May be I took the human form solely in commune
with you, as we both find ourselves here
between the two forces, good and evil.

(Ibidem)

The faith in God being absolute, Kumar sees life and eternity in their proper perspective. This is an oriental vision of life that baffles the mind of the occident. Kumar believes in the eternal presence of God before and after the creation and destruction of life and the world. Thus, he writes :

He was there before the Flood,
or after the Kurukshetra,
oblivious of all calamities —
shipwrecks, cyclones, eclipses — and
earthquakes that bring skyscrapers
to their knees, and carry temples
and brothels alike to the netherworld.

('Meditation')

One who understands this mystery of the Universe is a man of wisdom. He will repent all his misdeeds. Repentance is a human virtue without which one cannot even dream of redemption. Kumar not only sees life but understands it in all its facets — love, death, pain, suffering and isolation. That is why he lays emphasis on repentance in life. Confession of one's sins is not enough. It is repentance that purges one's sins and brings one closer to redemption. Thus, Kumar underlines the importance of repentance in the following words :

> But if confession, without penance
> could work, a parrot would claim
> rebirth as a bird of paradise.
>
> ('A Temple Atop a Hill')

Postcoloniality emphasizes a contemporary state and therefore, Kumar as a post-colonial poet writes poems of contemporary interest. He was for sometime, an expatriate Indian English poet in USA during his tenure as a distinguished Professor of English at the University of Oklahoma, Norman and at Franklin and Marshall College. Kumar is well versed with the new postcolonial terms like 'hybridity' and 'diaspora' and his poetry is a living example of these terms in action and operation. As Leela Gandhi has rightly pointed out that....

"Postcolonialism pursues a postnational reading of the colonial encounter by focussing on the global amalgam of cultures and identities consolidated by imperialism. To this end, it deploys a variety of conceptual terms and categories of analysis which examine the mutual contagion and subtle intimacies between coloniser and colonised. In this regard, the term 'hybridity' and 'diaspora,' in particular stand out for their analytic versatility and theoretical resilence" (1999 : 129).

Life at two ends of this world — one, in USA and another in India — is depicted in a touching poem 'A Letter to my Son.' The contrast is too glaring. As Kumar puts it :

> There, in Pittsburgh, it may now be snowing —
> the flakes blinding your window-pane....

But, here in Hyderabad, I have drawn the curtains
to dodge the sun's sanguine eye
glowering in its lethal anger.

After bringing out the contrast between the West and the East in geographical sense, he wants to show the contrast between childhood and youth and again between youth and old age and wants to dovetail the past into the present. Thus, he writes :

If only you could also skid back in time
to the summer morning that saw a yearling,
his tongue hanging like a puppy's, excited
over his first steps beyond the front gate
to face a new world....

You want me to fly out to you
on your American Express Card, as if it were a magic
carpet that could span both ends of a spectrum
heat and cold
youth and age

('A Letter to my Son')

One of the important traits of post-colonial poetry is that it successfully encounters reality in contemporary society through an ironic mode. Shiv K. Kumar himself underlines this aspect in the following words :

"What is truly distinctive about Post-Independence poetry (a synonymn for post-colonial poetry) is that it allows irony to play freely around all facets of human experience — social, religious, moral or political .... To the modern poet reality comes filtered through a juxtaposition of paradoxes" (1992 : 3).

Eunuchs are looked down upon in our society. The plight of eunuchs attract the attention of Kumar. He brings out the inherent contradiction in our society's attitude towards them. They are considered to be auspicious at the time of child birth and marriage — on these two occasions they are welcome but they remained cursed for ever. Thus, Kumar writes :

Between their cymbal-palms, the stray winds
break into song

> that brings you blessings from their gods
> who themselves died boonless.
>
> ('Eunuchs')

The irony in the last two lines turns out to be a kind of indictment of the society.

In another poem titled "A Subway Railway Station" (A Station Master's Monologue) Kumar takes a dig at the credulous nature of Indian people and exposes the hypocritical people. Thus, he writes :

> If only someone could plant a legend
> around that old banyan tree in the marketplace
> under which (let it be said) Sita dreamt
> of the golden deer, or that mammoth boulder
> behind which (let it be said) the Buddha picked up a viper
> and kissed its forked tongue out of compassion.
>
> (Woolgathering : 35)

Kumar then goes on to say that such an action will lead the credulous people to come to this place as pilgrims. Hence, the ironical ending :

> and the pilgrims come here
> in quest of the deer
> or the snake behind the boulder.
> And I'll hear the wedding bells!
>
> (A Subway Railway Station')

Kumar's texts are mostly 'indicative' texts (Raymond Williams' term) which indicate what is happening in the world. Kumar describes the things all around him — both at home and abroad. He sees things in their proper perspective and comes down heavily on such customs and rituals prevalent in the society with which he is not in agreement. His themes are post-colonial in texture for he makes an attempt to acclimatize an indigenous tradition and culture to English language. What is imbued in his themes is a form of resistance to the coloniser when he successfully avoided following the English literary tradition and gave a new dimension to Indian reality in his poetry. Ancient

Indian monuments, art and sculpture are brought into the realms of his poetry, for Kumar takes them an embodiment of creation. Thus, in "Khajuraho" he writes :

> Here the sculptor's hands
> have forged wanton patterns
> witnessed by bird, goat and priest
> as in every cosmic gyre
> the entire creation participates.

Apart from the themes, one important ingredient of post-colonial literature is the language (*i.e.*, the kind of English, not the Queen's English but 'other-englishes') in which it is written. Kumar's language (*i.e.*, the kind of English he uses) goes a longway to create a new Indian English idiom. The erotic vocabulary, the rhetoric and the new ways of measuring life in modern terms give a special quality to Kumar's poetry. He insists not only on saying new things but saying them in new ways. Thus, he asks :

> So, why this urge to relate
> to bird, flower and tree,
> to ache for love
> and grace? Aren't these only myths
> crucified in the scriptures?
>
> ("The Lemon Tree in my Backyard")

On the other hand, he describes the modern condition in the following words :

> We rest on treetops,
> eat the dust off sidewalks,
> slither into rat-holes.
>
> ('Thou Shalt not Commit')

Shiv K. Kumar as a post-colonial poet ranks favourably with major post-colonial poets both at home and abroad (*i.e*, in the Third World Countries). The themes of East-West encounter, transnationalism, hybridity, resistance to the former coloniser, and aboveall, the Indian English idiom give his poetry a distinct identity, called post-colonial poetry in the recent critical parlance.

WORKS CITED

Boehmer, Elleke. *Colonial and Postcolonial Literature.* Oxford : Oxford University Press, 1995.

Gandhi, Leela. *Postcolonial Theory : A Critical Introduction.* Delhi: OUP, 1999.

Hassan, Ihab. "Queries for Postcolonial Studies." *Journal of Literary Criticism.* 9 : 1 (June 2000) 25-37.

Kumar, Shiv K. *Contemporary Indian Literature.* New Delhi : Manohar Publications, (in collaboration with Indian Institute of Advanced Study, Shimla), 1992.

Rajnath. "Edward Said and Postcolonial Theory." *Journal of Literary Criticism* 9 : 1 (June 2000) 73-87.

Sabbu, Saraswati. "Shiv K. Kumar : An Interview." Rpt. *Journal of South Asian Literature* 25 : 2 Summer, Fall 1990.

6

Conclusion

After having discussed various aspects of Shiv K. Kumar's Poetry — themes, imagery, technique and idiom — it is imperative on my part to accord him the place he deserves on the map of post-colonial Indian English Poetry. His late arrival on the Indian English poetic scene (*i.e.*, in the nineteen seventies) notwithstanding, he has achieved and contributed a lot as a post-colonial Indian English poet and found a place in the first ever significant anthology of post-colonial Indian English poetry titled *Ten Twentieth Century Indian Poets* (OUP) along with nine other poets, edited by R. Parthasarathy in 1976. Like Jayanta Mahapatra he began writing poetry late in life (*i.e.*, in his fifties) and again, like Mahapatra, he too won the coveted Central Sahitya Akademi Award for his book of verse, *Trapfalls in the Sky* in 1987.

The question is : what's Kumar's contribution to post-colonial Indian English Poetry? The answer to this question leads to two further questions : (i) What significance has Kumar for the contemporary post-colonial Indian English poet? and (ii) Can he continue to be a source of inspiration to poets standing at the threshold of a new millennium? The answer to these questions is luckily for us in the affirmative.

I consider him as a great poet for reasons that are perfectly clear. He has courage of conviction, variety in themes, insight into the sufferings in life and aboveall, command of the language. He has adopted the post-colonial condition into the texture of his poetry.

Kumar's poetry begins in pain and sufferings in personal life but slowly it transcends the limitations of an individual's plight and acquires a greater significance for the readers in general. He moves away from the personal level to the social level and describes the injustice done to people at large in the name of religion, custom and superstion etc in our country. How to write poetry out of one's own sufferings in life was a problem for Kumar in the beginning of his poetic career and therefore, he turned to Robert Lowell and Sylvia Plath for inspiration. Here, is Kumar's confession :

"Let me make a confession that I have been influenced by Lowell and Plath from a thematic point of view. I mean a kind of confessionalism. The fact is that no work of art can create the right impact on the reader unless the thing is projected from your own personal experience. And that is where a kind of confessionalism has crept into my poetry. People have called me a confessional poet in that context, and to that extent I have been influenced by Lowell and Plath whose poetry, I admire. These are the people who have suffered crises, emotional, psychic, personal and it is to them I go to learn how poetry should be written" (*Literature and Criticism* 1991-2 : 151).

Kumar is in search of 'Prelapsarian innocence' (his own coinage) and therefore, he dislikes any kind of hypocrisy either in public or in personal life. Betrayal in love in personal life and hypocrisy of the priest in the social life are given enough space in his poetry. In his attitude to love and sex, and old age, Kumar is closer to W.B. Yeats. Like Yeats, Kumar does not think sex as unholy. One can achieve yogic concentration through pure sex but not the vulgar aspect of it. Kumar underlines his idea of sex in the following lines :

"Sex is a very vital part of our lives and must be included in writing, as long as the writer's treatment of sex does not become pornographic. I've always said that in our country we have Lord Venkateswara's temple and we also have Khajuraho. Our *Puranas* and *Shastras* are important, so is *Kama Sutra* which we have always recommended. When I introduce a woman in my writings, it is to show that sex need not be treated as something unclean. It is a very valid segment of human experience" (JSAL 25 : 2, 1990 : 232).

He further states :

"I have often been censored for being too open in portraying the sexual relationship between man and woman. But why should this central fact of life be camouflaged, treated hypocritically through oblique symbols and images. Sex should not be condemned if it is handled with grace, restraint, and sensitivity, and is not allowed to lapse into pornography. Our traditional art and culture always upheld the validity of both body and spirit. If our forefathers raised temples to our gods — Venkateshwara, Rama, or Krishna — they also immortalized the body through the great erotic sculptures at Khajuraho or Konarak. And haven't even our shastras blessed physical union between man and woman?" (Ibidem : 225).

Sex can also be sublime. Kumar reiterates this point :

"I think I am trying to make the same point, subconsciously though, when I make Eve speak out of her mind to Adam, in my poem "Eve to Adam" :

Shall I regret letting a stranger
hiss into my ears? I was always there
for you to decode my body, hear my
throat's birdsong. But we'd just lie
together alongside, like two sundered
boughs of the same tree.

And now this wanton urge
to bite the apples
off each other's breasts.

You, who were called upon to name
all cattle, bird and fish,
what beast is now crying out within me
for redemption"?

(Ibidem : 226)

With the advancing age, Kumar becomes conscious of the plight of the old age. Unlike any other post-colonial Indian English Poet, Kumar can be profitably read as a Poet of the old age. Poem after poem is *Woolgathering* Kumar harks on the plight of the old age. Here are a few examples :

Soon there'll be a gradual failure of the organs —
kidney, liver and the eyes —
for who can withstand the potency of darkness
which, like a polar bear, first carries its victim
deep into its lair
then licks him into sleep.

('Afternoon')

This is the moment
to recant
the pledge I'd made to an idol at a wayside shrine
to forget
the tree that had sheltered me against the acid-rain
to hide
my face behind the tombstone to muzzle my tears.
When I come to, I'll realize
that ripeness is a cruel mentor.

(Even at my Age ...)

Darkness, loneliness and quiet —
even though a stray stem of bougainvillea
keeps knocking at my window pane
as a gesture of fellowship.
My secrets I can leave to the owl's discretion —
he knows how much to hand out ...

If I have to fade away, let it happen now.
Soft footfalls down the hallway,
a gentle squeek of the front door
and a leap into the void,
leaving the last rites to be done
by the day which has savoured neither understanding
nor solitude — only words
that stutter and groan.

('Night')

Marble graves are for the scion
of royalty — roses and lilies —
not for the commoners who are swept off by history
into a mass grave, where they lie for centuries
till they become manure for the new-born

('A Requiem for Autumn Leaves')

The above quotations reinforce Kumar's idea of old age and a mental preparedness to accept life on life's terms. His lines make us see reality and that is the hall mark of good poetry. Kumar's observation, "ripeness is a cruel mentor," a variation on Shakespeare's magic words, 'ripeness is all,' is an apt commentary on post-colonial condition. He puts down no shutters and puts on no blinkers — however difficult it may be, Kumar does not wish to run away from harsh realities of life. He seeks to restore innocence in life, his bitter personal experiences not withstanding.

In the manner of T.S. Eliot, Kumar has incorporated into the texture of his poetry a good deal of worldly wisdom and robust commonsense. As a result, his poetry becomes a repository of knowledge derived from experience and intuition. Here, are a few examples.

Father mumbles in his dream :
Read the *Gita*. Take both light
and shade with the equipoise
of a call girl.
Easier said than done.

('Stress')

In the beginning was the cry,
not the word. But didn't it sound
like a loud protest against what was to follow?
Time's assault on innocence.

('Birth of my Son')

But if confession, without penance
could work, a parrot would claim
rebirth as a bird of paradise

('A Temple Atop a Hill')

The way inside is the wayout
to understanding —
that each paradox carries two faces :
bud and insect, beginning and end.

("Meditation")

Pain, he has now learnt, is born
in the mother's womb, and ends only
when the ashes are silenced

('Renunciation')

The echoes of Eliot and Shakespeare are unmistakable.

In Kumar's poetry there is a sustained growth and development both in theme and technique — he has come a longway from *Articulate Silences* (1970) to *Thus Spake the Buddha* (forthcoming) — from disillusionment to realisation. There is a progression in his poetry in terms of broadening of one's consciousness of the trials and tribulations of life. For Kumar, Life is not a song to be sung but a challenge to be faced — however hurt he may feel, he does not shun reality. Like Keats he wants to release his own sorrows, pain and sufferings through poetry. He has an open mind and liberal outlook. He distrusts any kind of ideology in life and believes in 'free living and free thinking.'

As a post-colonial Indian English Poet Kumar deals with national and transnational themes with an open mind. Poverty, superstition, injustice, hypocrisy double-dealing, failure in married life, and betrayal in life in the contemporary society — all come within the purview of his poetry. Sufferings in personal life and sufferings in the society at large make him sad and he exposes those who are responsible for the sufferings of the common people. As he concentrates on contemporary situation, he shuns the use of myths in his poetry. He does not glorify the tradition, on the other hand, he lays emphasis on contemporary reality. The whole country (*i.e.*, the whole of India) becomes the locale of his poetry — a priest of Varanasi, a crematorium at Hyderabad, the pavement sleepers in Bombay, a temple in Calcutta, women at the village wells anywhere in the country and the death of a foreign missionary in Orissa etc. — come within the purview of his searching eye and he writes animatedly about them. Kumar depicts the sad incident of an Australian Missionary, Graham Staines' death in a poem titled 'Murder of a Missionary' in a tone imbued with pathos. The humanist in Kumar is clearly seen in the following lines :

> Sundown. A van carrying him and his two sons
> is torched. A frantic struggle to escape
> but they're speared back into the inferno.
> An anguished sky blazes a forked lightning
> to signal the end of innocence.
> ...
> when the media flashed his photograph,
> he looked like a prophet who'd walked
> over the Pacific waters, all the way
> from his land of Kangaroo, to seek
> crucifixion far away from home.

This poem can also be taken as an example of Kumar's transnationalism in which he laments the death of a foreigner and his two sons in our country.

This kind of brutality in society causes depression in the mind of the poet, who is in the autumn of his life. The agony of the lost innocence abides. Thus, he writes in a poem titled, 'Depression.'

> It comes and goes.
> Like some ominous tidal wave
> that hits a lone island
> far beyond the sea's ramparts.
>
> A kite cut loose from its string
> swings idly, upside down,
> in the autumn wind.
> ...
> No footfalls anywhere,
> only a void that resembles Yama
> in *The Book of the Dead.*
> How long would this last?

The agony of life, the suffering from within, makes the poet sad but wise, as he is now able to see into the mystery of life. There is a note of rebellion that comes from within which leads to a kind of self-questioning in a poem called, "General Ward, Osmania Hospital." As Kumar puts it :

> If pain and existence are like two sides
> of the same medallion (as says, Ghalib)
> then why toll temple bells,
> bathe deities in cow's milk
> and pray for the life of a banyan tree?
>
> We forget that at sundown
> we'll be led through a subway to a cellar
>
> Where mummies lie, cheek by jowl,
> dreaming of immortality.

Like Eliot and Ezekiel in their last phase of poetic career, Kumar is a humanistic poet, sympathizing with suffering humanity as he advances in age and acquires wisdom. He now realises that 'only after malice and revenge have lost their string,' the heart will be ready 'for redemption.'

Apart from employing new themes in his poetry, Kumar has contributed substantially to the creation of a new idiom (*i.e.*, Indian English idiom) and a new kind of 'other englishes' which is a precondition for post-colonial poetry. Kumar's vocabulary is learned like the vocabularly of English Metaphysical poets. His fondness for similes and metaphors, irony and paradox is remarkable. He has a knack for neolism and therefore, one encounters a number of interesting coinages in his poetry. Here are a few examples :

'Colonial moustache,' 'sabre eyes,' 'fugitive cloud,' 'self-righteous coconuts,' 'scimitar-tongue,' 'virgin transparency,' 'ancestral memories,' 'clipped syllabus,' 'splintered tongues,' 'womb of time,' 'exotic chant,' 'choleric air,' 'hybrid moon,' 'champagned ripples,' 'forespent thighs' , 'monolithic rocks,' 'mango ripples,' 'sophomore breasts,' etc. Kumar's innovative images are startling and they make an assertion of the novelty of expression by a postcolonial poet. Landscape is an important ingredient of post-colonial poetry and therefore, many post-colonial poets integrate it with the people of the place. Like Nissim Ezekiel, and Keki N. Daruwalla, Shiv K. Kumar too integrates the landscape of the place with the people and thereby, depicts reality that confronts them. One is reminded of two important poems of Kumar in this context : they are "Dawnbreak over Khasi Hills' and "Walking by the River side." Kumar describes :

> Out there, from the drowsy valley
> rises a wail, bemoaning all those tribal
> ancestors who walked away beyond the hills,
> centuries ago,
> lost in their secret sorrows.
>
> ('Dawnbreak over Khasi Hills')
>
> And, perhaps, there still lies at the foot
> of the neem tree, near the river's bend,
> that white round pebble on which my fancy
> etched a word more resonant than Om,
> while a sanguine figure learned out of the clouds
> to caution me :
>
> disaster comes too soon to those
> who converse with water at dusk
> when the blood loses its immunity
> against amnesia
> and the past and present eddy around each other
> reinforcing nothingness.
>
> ("Walking by the Riverside")

If transnationalism and multicultural encounters are some of the ingredients of postcolonial poetry, Kumar has little to fear. He has written a number of poems including a full section 'Under Alien Skies' (seven poems) in *Trapfalls in the Sky*. The innovative images and the implicit irony make the poems in 'Under Alien Skies' section stimulating and vibrant. Here are some examples :

> The white raven, perched on a high
> stool behind his magic book,

can caw off the names
of all your ancestors
like the panda on the Ganges bank.

You'll break through the sound
barrier only if your dart hits
the god's eye. Otherwise, the silver
trawlers flying the royal ensign may
whirl you back to your genesis

("Heathrow Airport : Immigration Checkpost.")

Done with Cambridge, I let a train
disgorge me at Liver Pool street,
East Ends. Blindfolded by the late autumn
smog, the sun gropes for an exist.
...
In the shop-windows of Bond Street
the mannequins, draped in virgin
transparency, grin at my jadded
loins. Farther down the street
a salvation band, its conductor
a Tussaud's waxen colonel, strikes
up a hymn :

'Go ye into this wilderness
to seek thy damnation!'

('A Reminiscence')

Comparison between the officials at Imigration check post and pandas on the Ganges bank is an intersting one. Kumar's sense of irony and humour is commendable. Again the sun being 'blindfolded by late autumn smog' is an apt and innovative image. Kumar's collocation of words, use of imagery and aboveall creation of new Indian English idiom make him a successful post-colonial poet.

While concluding, I would like to come back to the two questions I have posed in the beginning of this chapter : (i) what significance has Kumar for contemporary post-colonial Indian English poet? and (ii) can he continue to be a source of inspiration to poets standing at the threshold of a new millennium? and make my assessment of him as a post-colonial poet. To my mind, Kumar's significance as a post-colonial. Indian English poet lies in his employment of new themes and images in his poetry. His poetry is both an assertion of nationalism and transnationalism. He has deromanticised images — sun/moon/sky, etc. in his poetry. He has also shown the way as to how one can create poetry out of his own sufferings in life without making it banal. There may be many a Freudian slip in his poetry but his poetry transcends the limitations of an individual's loss and gain and becomes a vehicle for the expression of the aspiration of common man. There is a search for innocence and urge for artistic honesty in his poetry which go a long way to establish the authenticity of it. A good poet/writer is one who creates or re-creates authentic characters in their situation. Kumar's characters be it a cabaret dancer, a priest, an aspiring poet, a mango vendor, a woman labourer, a pavement sleeper or a betrayed lover/husband — all come alive in his poetry. There is a sense of immediacy and transparency in his poetry. He shows the way as to how to write poetry being true to one's own experience. Like Nissim Ezekiel, and Kamala Das, he gives a very daring portrayal of love and sex in his poetry. Love and sex are an integral part of life and in order to accept art, one has to affirm sensuality. For Kumar sex when treated artistically becomes a life giving force, but he never advocates unclean sex. Consummation of love and sex is always welcome, if it leads to procreation. Is not it Eliot who said, "What you get married for if you don't want children?"

Kumar will always be a source of inspiration for Indian English poets in the new millennium for his daring portrayal of new themes in straight forward language. His courage of conviction in choosing a language (*i.e.*, English) other than his mother tongue (*i.e.*, Punjabi) as the medium of creative expression and disapproval of choosing any language for parochial consideration will always inspire the new poets. Moreover, as a post-colonial Indian English poet he does not speak for any particular region or community or glorify any particular tradition, on the other hand, he speaks for the whole of India. His pan Indian sensibility and outlook endear him to the readers all over the country. Like any sensible post-colonial poet anywhere in the world, Kumar believes in revising a poem. An artist, like a woman must labour to be beautiful. Kumar believes in this maxim and writes poetry with utmost sincerity to his own sensibility and choice of idioms. To some readers, his poetry may appear difficult in the matter of diction and collocation of words but the profit of reading Kumar's poetry is a 'mind expanding delight.' To read his poetry is to realize and 'see' the contemporary reality in our country. The poet who began his poetic career under the shadow and agony of his mother's death and his own traumatic divorce, has now come to realize that 'attachment generates only anguish.' A wiser poet now knows that beyond human consciousness, 'there is the essence of perennial tranquillity' and therefore, he wants to live in harmony as our sages did two millennia ago, 'with the wind, rain, thunder — and the beasts.' Kumar's poetry which began in pain and moved in passion, has become a tragic affirmation of life. This is an achievement that has not been equalled by many post-colonial poets in our time.

WORKS CITED

Asnani, Shyam. "Interview with Shiv K. Kumar," *Literature and Criticism* 1 : 1-2, 1991-92.

Sabbu, Saraswati. Rpt. "Shiv K. Kumar : An Interview." *Journal of South Asian Literature* 25 : 2 Summer, Fall 1990.

Select Bibliography

Primary Sources

Kumar, Shiv K. *Articulate Silences*. Calcutta : Writers' Workshop, 1970.

———. *Cobwebs in the Sun*. New Delhi : Tata McGraw-Hill, 1974.

———. *Subterfuges*. New Delhi : Oxford University Press, 1976.

———. *Woodpeckers*, London : Sidgwick and Jackson, 1979.

———. *Trapfalls in the Sky*, Madras : Macmillan, 1986.

———. *Woolgathering*. Mumbai : Disha Books, 1998.

———. *Thus Spake the Buddha* (forthcoming).

Secondary Sources : Articles

Aikant, Satish C. "Dilemma of Nationalism : Siting Postcolonial Theory," *Journal of Literary Criticism* 8 : 2, December 1996 : 70-80.

Alexander, Meena. "Exiled by a Dead Script," *The Journal of Indian Writing in English*. 5.2, 1977, 1-4.

Amanuddin, Syed. "Love and Sex in Indo-English Poetry," *Creative Moment III : I Spring* 1974.

Anniah Gowda, H.H. "A Defence of Indian Verse in English," *The Literary Half-Yearly*. 9.2, 1968, 23-376.

———. "Contemporary Creative Writers in India," *The Literary Half-Yearly*. 10.1, Jan. 1969, 17-39.

———. "The Use of Images in Contemporary, Indian Verse in English," WLWE, 20. 1971, 61-76.

Birje Patil, J. "Resonant Bones : The Poetry of Shiv K. Kumar," *World Literature Today*, 51, No. 4, Autumn 1977, 543-548.

Bose, Amalendu. "Some Poets of the Writers' Workshop, *Critical Essays on Indian Writing in English.* Eds. M.K. Naik *et al.*, Dharwar : Karnatak University, 1968, 31-50.

———. "Modern Indian Poetry in English," *Indian Literature*, 13, 1 March, 1970, 51-59.

Bose, B. "Indian Poetry in English," *The Concise Encyclopaedia of English and American Poets and Poetry.* Eds. S. Spender and D. Hall. London : Hutchinson and Co. 1963, 142-143.

Chatterjee, Usasi. "Twenty Five years of Indo-English Poetry." *Review of Indian Poetry in English*, 1947-72. Ed. Pritish Nandy. Indian and Foreign Review 1, February, 1973, 8.

Chellappan, K. "Irony as Understanding and Love in Three Indo-Anglian Poets," *Journal of Literature and Aesthetics.* 11 : 4, October, 1982, 36-40.

Chitre, Dilip. "Poetry in the Enemy's Tongue," *New Quest* 14 March-April, 1979, 77-82.

Das, Bijay Kumar. "Aspects of Modern Indian Poetry in English." *The Indian Journal of English Studies*, Vol. XX, No. 1, 1980, 39-50.

———. "Some Indian English Poets of the Seventies," *Indian Literature*, 25, 3 May-June 1982, 101-109.

———. "Indian Poetry in English," *The Illustrated Weekly of India*, 27 June, 1982, 28-29.

———. "Ironic Mode in Modern Indo-English Poetry," *Journal of Literature and Aesthetics*, 11.4 1982, 75-82.

———. "Indo-English poetry to Recent years," *Poetry V.* 1983, 32-39.

———. "Recent Indian Poetry in English," *The Literary Half-Yearly.* 25. 1, 1984, 52-58.

———. "The Love Poetry of Kamala Das and Shiv K. Kumar : A Comparative Study." *The Mahanadi Review* 4 : 1, 1985.

———. "Indian Landscape and Imagery in the poetry of Shiv K. Kumar." *Creative Forum.* 1.1, 1988.

———. "Indian English Poetry : Before and After Independence," *Triveni*, 56, 3 and 4.

———. "The Crystal Glance of Love : Kamala Das and Shiv K. Kumar as Love Poets." *Love and Death in Indian Poetry in English*. Ed. S.N.A. Rizvi. New Delhi : Doaba House, 1989.

———. "The Image of the 'Native Land' in the Award Winning Poets," *Chiaroscuro* (ed.) A.S. Ratnam, Parbhani : Phynanopasak prakashan, 1991.

———. "Trends in Post-colonial Poetry," *The Critical Endeavour*, 4, 1998.

———. "Akademi Award Winning Indian English Poetry as Post-Colonial Text," *Critical Practice* 6 : 2 1999.

Dulai, Surjit S. "Shiv K. Kumar's Writing," *Journal of South Asian Literature*, 25 : 2, Summer, Fall 1998, 9-48.

Dwivedi, A.N. "Irony as Technique in some new Indo-English Poets," *JLA*, 2, 4, 83-94.

Harrex, S.C. "Small-Scale Reflections on Indian English Language Poetry," *Journal of Indian Writing in English*, Vol. VIII, 1-2, 1980, 137-166.

Hess, Linda. "Post-Independence Indian Poetry in English" *Quest* 49, April-June, 28-38.

Iradate, Roger. "Indian Poetry in English To-day," *Quest* 98, Nov-Dec, 1975, 72-74.

Iyengar, K.R. Srinivas. "Indian Poetry in English : Yesterday, Today, Tomorrow," *The Literary Criterion*, 18.3, 1983, 10-18.

Jaggi, Satya Dev. "Indo-English Poetry in the Context of World Standard," *Journal of Indian Writing in English*, 1.1, 1973, 35-38.

Kaul, R.K. "An Essay on the Poems of Shiv K. Kumar," *Osmania Journal of English Studies*, 11 : 1, 1974-75, 62-68.

Kohli, Devindra. "Passionate sincerity in Indian Poetry in English," *Journal of Commonwealth Literature*, 9, 1, (August 1974) 20-34.

Kohli, Suresh. "Indian Poetry in English," *The Indian Literary Review*, 1. No. 7-8, (Nov. Dec. 1978) 33-40.

Kulshrestha, Chirantan. "English Verse in India : Some Obstinate Questions," *Contemporary Indian English Verse* : An Evaluation, New Delhi : Arnold Heinemann, 1980, 9-19.

Mahapatra, Jayanta. "The Inaudible Resonance in English Poetry in India," *The Literary Criterion*, 15. 1, 1980 : 27-36.

———. "The Decline of Indian English Poetry," *The Journal of Indian Writing in English*. 28 : 1 Jan., 2000, 3-6.

Mahashabde, N.C. "Indian Poetry in English," *Quest 50*, July-Sept., 1966, 110.

McCutchion, David. "Must Indian Poetry in English Always Follow England?" *Critical Essays on Indian Writing in English*. Ed., M.K. Naik, *et al.,* (Dharwar : Karnatak University, 1968) 164-180.

Mukhopadhya, Durga Das. "Review of S.K. Kumar's 'Cobwebs in the Sun,'" *Mini Max*, 1975, 24-35.

Nabar, Vrinda. "The Critical Imperative in Indo-English Poetry," *Cygnus*, 2.1, 1980, 33-39.

Naik, M.K. "The Indianness of Indian Poetry in English," *Journal of Indian Writing in English*, 1.2, July 1973, 1-7.

———. "Echo and Voice in Indian Poetry in English," *Indian Writing To-day*, 4.1, 1970, 32-41.

———. "The Achievement of Indian English Poetry," *The Humanities Review* 4.1 and 2, Jan. - Dec., 1982, 22-29.

Nandy, Pritish. "Indian Poetry in English : The Dynamics of New Sensibility," *Indian Literature*, 14.1, 1972, 8-12.

Nandakumar, Prema. "An Interview with Prof. Shiv. K. Kumar," *The Indian Express*, 7 Jan., 1977, p-3.

Narayan, Shyamala. A "Review of Ten Twentieth Century Indian Poets." Ed. R. Parthasarathy. *World Literature Today*, 52.1, Winter 1978, 180.

Nayak, Pramod K. "Poetry of the Nineties," *Chandrabhaga* 1/2000, 95-119.

Padhi, Bibhu Prasad. "The Parallel Voice : A Study of the New English Poetry in India : Quest 98," Nov-Dec., 1975, 37-46.

Paniker, K. Ayyappa. "Peacocks Among Patriarch : A Close Look at Indian Poetry in English," *New Quest*, 2, August 1977, 59-70.

———. "Indian Poetry in English and the Indian Aesthetic Tradition," *The Indian Journal of English Studies*, 23, 1983, 137-151.

Paranjape, Makarand. "The State of Poetry : Reflections on the Changing Identity of Indian English Verse." *Chandrabhaga* 2/2000 : 66-88.

Perry, John Oliver. "On Seeking an Appropriately Multicultural Criticism for Indian Literatures." *Chandrabhaga* 2/2000 : 91-103.

Parashar, B.P. "Aesthetics of Irony in Shiv K. Kumar," *Journal of Literature and Aesthetics*, 2 : 4, October, 1982, 41-52.

Parthasarathy, R. "Indian English Verse : The Making of a Tradition." *The Humanist Review*, 1. 1, July-Sept., 1979, 5-8.

———. "Tradition and Freedom," *The Indian Journal of English Studies*, Vol. XXI, 1981-82, 47-59.

Rayan, Krishna. "Contemporary Indian English Poetry and the Gods." *Chandrabhaga*. 1/2000. 43-52.

———. "Aesthetics of Irony in Modern Indo-English Poetry," *Journal of Literature and Aesthetics*, 2. 4, October 1982, 28-35.

Sivaram Krishna, M. "Beyond the Empiric Point : Poetry of Shiv K. Kumar," *World Literature Written in English* 14. 2, Nov. 1975, 371-384.

———. "Contemporary Indian Poetry in English : An Approach," *Opinion Literary Quarterly*, 1. 4, July, 1974, 39-57.

Srinath, C.N. "Contemporary Indian Poetry in English," *The Literary Criterion*, 8. 2, 55-56.

Srivastava, A.K. and Smita Sinha. "New Voices : Animad Versions on Recent Indo-Anglian Poetry," *Indian Writing in English*. Ed. K.N. Sinha. New Delhi : Heritage Publishers, 1979, 109-127.

Shivastava, R.C. "Articulating the Silent : The Poetry of Shiv. K. Kumar," *The Journal of India Writing in English*, 6. 2, 1978, 1-12.

Tambimutta. "Poetry in India : Its Heritage and New Directions," *Atlantic Monthly* 192, No. 4, 147-148.

Vaidyanathan, T.G. "Between Kali and Cordelia : The Poetry of Shiv. K. Kumar," *Osmania Journal of English Studies*, 13. 1, 1977, 61-83.

Venkatachari, K. "Towards an Idiom of Sincerity : A Study of the Poetry of Shiv K. Kumar," *The Journal of Indian Writing in English*, 4. 2, July, 1976, 52-58.

———. "Indian Poetry in English Today," *Indian P.E.N.*, 40. 2-3, Feb-March, 1974, 1-6.

Walsh, William. "The Indian Poets," *The Literary Criterion*, 11 : 3, Winter 1974, 1-6.

———. "Small Observations on a Large Subject," *Aspects of Indian Writing in English*. Ed. M.K. Naik, Delhi : Macmillan and Co., 1979, 107-119.

Anthologies and Books

Abidi, S.Z.H. *Studies in Indo-Anglian Poetry*. Bareilly : Prakash Book Depot, 1978.

Ahmad, Aijaz. *In Theory : Classes, Nations, Literatures*. New Delhi : Oxford University Press, 1992.

Amanuddin, Syed. *World Poetry in English*, New Delhi : Sterling Publishers, 1981.

Bharucha, Nilufer E. and Vrinda Nabar. Eds. *Mapping Cultural Spaces : Post-colonial Indian Literature in English*. New Delhi : Vision Books, 1998.

Boehmer, Elleke. *Colonial and Postcolonial Literature*. Oxford : Oxford University Press, 1995.

Das, Bijay Kumar. *Modern Indian English Poetry*. Bareilly : Prakash Book Depot, 1992.

———. *Critical Essays on Poetry*, New Delhi : Kalyani Publishers, 1993.

———. *Aspects of Commonwealth Literature*. New Delhi : Creative Books, 1995.

———. *A Reader's Guide to Ten Twentieth Century Indian Poets*. Bareilly : Prakash Book Depot, 1997.

———. *Critical Essays on Post-colonial Literature*. New Delhi : Atlantic Publishers and Distributors, 1999.

———. Ed. *Contemporary Indo-English Poetry*. Bareilly : Prakash Book Depot, 1986.

Deshpande, Gauri. Ed. *An Anthology of Indo-English Poetry*, New Delhi : Hind Pocket Books, 1974.

Dweivedi, A.N. *Indo-Anglian Poetry*, Allahabad : Kitab Mahal, 1979.

———. Ed. *Indian Poetry in English : A Literary History and Anthology*, New Delhi : Arnold Heinemann, 1980.

Gandhi, Leela. *Postcolonial Theory : A Critical Introduction*. Delhi : Oxford University Press, 1999.

Gokak, V.K. Ed. *The Golden Treasury of Indo-Anglian Poetry* New Delhi : Sahitya Akademi, 1970.

———. Ed. *Studies in Indo-Anglian Poetry*. Bangalore : Sairatan Agency, 1972.

Iyengar, K.R. Srinivasa. *Indo-Anglian Literature*. Bombay : International Book House, 1943.

———. *Indian Writing in English*. New Delhi : Sterling Publishers, 1984.

———. *Two Cheers for the Commonwealth*. Bombay : Asia Publishing House, 1970.

Jain, Jasbir and Veena Singh. Ed. *Contesting Postcolonialism*. Jaipur : Rawal Publications, 2000.

Jussawalla, Adil. Ed. *New Writing in English*, Harmonds. worth : Penguin Books, 1974.

Karnani, Chetan. *Indian Writing in English*. New Delhi : Arnold Associates, 1995.

King, Bruce. *Modern Indian Poetry in English*. New Delhi : Oxford University Press, 1987.

Kotoky, P.C. *Indo-English Poetry*. Gauhati : Gauhati University, Department of Publication, 1969.

Kulshrestha, Chirantan. Ed. *Contemporary Indian English Verse : An Evaluation*. New Delhi : Arnold Heinemann, 1980.

Kumar, Shiv K. *Contemporary Indian Literature in English*. New Delhi : Manohar Publications, 1992.

Lal, P. Ed. *Indian Writing in English : A Symposium*. Calcutta, Writers' Workshop, 1961.

McCutchion, David. *Indian Writing English : Critical Essays*. Calcutta : Writers' Workshop, 1969.

Mehrotra, Arvind Krishna. Ed. *The Oxford India Anthology of Twelve Modern Indian Poets*. Delhi : Oxford University Press, 1998.

Mohan, Ramesh. Ed. *Indian Writing in English*. Madras : Orient Longman, 1978.

Mongia, Padmini. Ed. *Contemporary Postcolonial Theory*. New Delhi : Oxford University Press, 1997.

Naik, M.K. Ed. *Aspects of Indian Writing in English*. New Delhi : MacMillan, 1979.

———. *Dimensions of Indian English Literature*. New Delhi : Sterling Publishers, 1984.

———. *A History of Indian English Literature*. New Delhi, Sahitya Akademi, 1982.

———. *Studies in Indian English Literature*. New Delhi : Sterling Publishers, 1987.

———. *Perspectives on Indian Poetry in English*. New Delhi : Abhinav Publications, 1984.

Naik, M.K. *et al*. *Critical Essays on Indian Writing in English*. Dharwar : Karnatak University, 1968.

Nandy, Pritish. *Indian Poetry in English Today*. New Delhi : Sterling, 1973.

Narasimhaiah, C.D. *The Swan and the Eagle*. Simla : Indian Institute of Advanced Study, 1969.

———. *Essays in Commonwealth Literature : Heirloom of Multiple Heritage*. Delhi : Pencraft International, 1995.

Paranjape, Makarand. *Mysticism in Indian English Poetry*. Delhi : B.R. Publications, 1988.

Parthasarathy, R. Ed. *Ten Twentieth Century Indian Poets*. New Delhi : Oxford University Press, 1977.

Pathak, R.S. Ed. *Creative Forum* (Special Issue : Quest for Identity in Indian English Poetry) V Jan.-December '92.

Peeradina, Saleem. Ed. *Contemporary Indian Poetry in English : An Assessment and Selection*. Bombay : MacMillan, 1972.

Paniker, K. Ayyappa. Ed. *Indian English Literature since Independence*. New Delhi : The Indian Association for English Studies, 1991.

Perry, John Oliver. *Absent Authority : Issues in Contemporary Indian English Criticism*. New Delhi : Sterling Publishers, 1992.

Prasad, G.J.V. *Continuities in Indian English Poetry*. New Delhi : Pencraft International, 1999.

Raghava Charyulu, D.V.K. *The Two Fold Voice : Essays on Indian Writing in English* : Vijayawada : Navodaya Publishers, 1971.

Rajan, P.K. Ed. *Changing Traditions in Indian English Literature*. New Delhi : Creative Books, 1995.

Ramaswamy, S. *Explorations : Essays on Commonwealth Literature*. Bangalore : MCC Publications, 1988.

Reddy, G.A. *Indian Writing in English and Its' Audience*. Bareilly : Prakash Book Depot, 1978.

Rizvi, S.N.A. Ed. *Love and Death in Indian Poetry in English*. Delhi : Doaba House, 1989.

Saha, Subhas. *Modern Indo-Anglian Love-Poetry*. Calcutta : Workshop 1971.

Sarang, Vilas. Ed. *Indian English Poetry since 1950 : An Anthology*. Bombay : Disha Books, 1995.

Seshadri, P. *Anglo-Indian Poetry*. Banaras. Indian Book-shop, 1928.

Shahane, Vasant A. and Sivaram Krishna, M. Ed. *Indian Poetry in English : A Critical Assessment*. Madras : MacMillan, 1982.

Sharma, K.K., Ed. *Indo-English Literature*. Ghaziabad : Vimal Prakashan, 1977.

Sinha, K.N. *Indian Writing in English*. New Delhi : Heritage Publishers, 1979.

Trivedi, Harish and Meenakhi Mukherjee. Eds. *Interrogating Post-colonialism : Theory, and Text and Context*. Shimla : Indian Institute of Advanced Study, 1996.

Varma, Monika. *Facing Four Indo-Anglian Poetess*. Calcutta : Writers' Workshop, 1973.

Verghese, C. Paul. *Essays on Indian Writing in English*. New Delhi : N.V. Publishers, 1975.

William, Walsh. *Readings in Commonwealth Literature*. Oxford Clarendon Press, 1973.

———. *Commonwealth Literature*. London : Oxford University Press, 1973.

———. *Indian Literature in English*. London : Longman, 1990.

Williams, H.M. *Indo-Anglian Literature* 1800-1970 : *A Survey*. Madras : Orient Longman, 1970.

Index

Postscript

Losing my Way : This is the eighth book of poems by Shiv K. Kumar scheduled to be published early next year (*i.e.*, in 2002). Since some of the poems are very interesting, I would like to make an overview of them in this book. Hence, the postscript.

Kumar as I have shown in the concluding chapter of this book has become a humanistic poet, like Eliot in his "Little Gidding" and Ezekiel in his *Collected Poems* 1952-88. Kumar has acquired in the fag end of his poetic career the Shakespearean wisdom embodied in the line 'forget and forgive' (Lear's words to Cordelia). Shakespearean wisdom and Eliotian humility have great appeal to Kumar at his ripe old age of 'fourscore and more.' Hence, he writes some of the most outstanding poems in this volume (*i.e.*, *Losing My Way*) which speak to us about the essence of life on earth.

Kumar turns to the *Mahabharat* (particularly to the *Gita*, the repository of human wisdom) in a poem called "Bhishampitama to Yudhister Dharamaraj" to make us aware of certain basic truths of life.

Thus, he writes :

> Yes, Yudhister, it's only through pain's eye that you can perceive truth. How unfortunate are those who see only the rainbow, hear only the spring's melody, and dream on a cloud's thistledown bed. The way to see is to go blind, the way to fly is to crawl on your belly.

The Mss. of *Losing My Way* has been finalised very recently and made available to me by the Poet.

The paradox in the last two lines quoted above is imbued with wisdom. To know oneself is not egoism for it leads to understand life better than ever before. It is suffering which not only helps one to see into the mysteries of life but makes him/her more human. Kumar rightly underlines the value of experience in life when he says, that "experience's voice is more authentic/than even divinity's." This poem can be read as a sequel to "Lord Krishna to Arjuna" (included in his seventh book of poems, *Thus Spake the Buddha*) for it reinforces the ideas and wisdom embodied in that poem. As Kumar puts it :

> Karma! Action divorced from all thoughts of recompense...
> Disinterested action — that's sit.
> Why should be mortals alone ache for the
> fruits of their action? Holding an act ransom to
> result. That way lies pain. Sun or moon, drought
> or rain, sickness or health — this equipoise alone
> can bring one to peace, anywhere at the oceans
> buttom or atop Mount Kailash.

Kumar lays emphasis on the doctrine of Karma which if understood rightly will bring peace to one's mind.

Time moves on and God is the unmoved mover. Success or failure, ignorance, defeat or revelation the wheel of time moves on. That is an eternal truth of life.

Thus, Kumar says :

> Retreat and revelation. The wheel
> Keeps turning.
>
> ('The Sun's Eye')

Even then, people cannot easily rise above greed and avarice. For such people who succumb to temptation, Kumar has a suggestion though not without gentle irony as stated in a poem titled, "Feeding the Pigeons." Kumar writes :

> Sly are the ways of temptation.
> Birds with grains, children with choc-bars,
> brunettes with bracelets.

After saying this Kumar seeks to bring home the truth of success in regard to possessing something in life. Thus, he concludes the poem :

> The way to hold is to keep one's palm open.
> The way to possess is not to grab.

One can get one's heart's desire cherished through love. The best way to possess is not to possess by desire but by love. This is a truth felt in the pulse and felt along the heart. Kumar has acquired the wisdom of an old man and wants to share it with the readers through his poetry. That is why,

Kumar's poetry as I have stated in the concluding chapter has become 'a mind expanding delight.'

Art of writing poetry has been a major obsession with modern poets, post-modern poets and post-colonial poets for quite sometime. From Yeats and Eliot to the closing of the twentieth century, most of the poets are revising their poems as a rule. For some a poem is never complete, it is abandoned. It is a well established fact that poets borrow from several sources (themes and images etc.) and write poetry making use of their borrowings. Even great poets like Chaucer, Shakespeare and Eliot are no exceptions. Kumar, a distinguished Professor of English and a scholar and a critic of repute, brings to his poetry all his learnings from English literature, literatures in English and several other sources. He makes no secret of it. But he candidly tells us how a poem is written in the following words :

> Words are straws picked up
> by a sparrow, from everywhere :
> rose-garden, roadside, even dustbin
> Butif the beak and eye have a vision,
> they'd embroider them into the
> pattern of a nest which may sing
> like a poem even when nobody's around.
>
> ('Birth of a Poem')

Like a sparrow building a nest collecting straws from several sources, a poet too builds his poem borrowing words and images from several sources. If a poet has insight into human nature, he can create good poems which will transcend the limitations of time and place. Kumar is hinting at intertexutuality, as advocated by the post-structuralist critics. It is in this sense (*i.e.*, the critical approach) that Kumar's poetry can be read as postcolonial poetry. The title poem of his forthcoming book of verse, *Losing My Way* can be read profitably at the deep structure level. It's an oblique poem which shows the insight of Kumar as a true contemporary poet. At one level, it can be read as a poem showing the dilemma in the minds of an expatriate poet, who wants to return home because he does not feel at home abroad. The English language the poet had learnt at home is sadly inadequate to communicate with the native speakers of English abroad. Moreover, the city life there is vastly different from the Indian condition and hence the discomfort. Kumar re-creates this situation in a lively way in the following lines :

> I've lost my way
> in this strange city —
> far away from home
>
> Each hour they change
> their street signs and carry
> their traffic signs away
> Down the dark alley ways.
>
> I learnt their language before
> coming here. But they've tampered
> its syntax and banished all its vowels
> So how shall I communicate?

This is how R. Parthasarathy felt when he went to London and wanted to return home as expressed in his wellknown poem, *Rough Passage.*

Similarly Kumar feels like a fish out of water there and wants to return home. Thus, he writes :

I wanna go home
before I'm houn'ded out.
I wanna sleep on my mother's lap.
She's calling me
From across the seas
I'm done.

Kumar's love for his mother is the driving force behind his poetry. The love for the mother and motherland helps him to assume an identity independent of his stay in foreign lands. Thus, he writes back to the empire, an important ingredient of post-colonial poetry. His latest forthcoming book of verse, *Losing My Way* affirms Kumar's position as a post-colonial poet par excellence.